THE ABOLITION

JONATHAN SCHELL

Other Avon Books by
Jonathan Schell

THE FATE OF THE EARTH

THE
ABOLITION

JONATHAN
SCHELL

AVON
PUBLISHERS OF BARD, CAMELOT, DISCUS AND FLARE BOOKS

The contents of this book originally appeared in *The New Yorker*.

AVON BOOKS
A division of
The Hearst Corporation
1790 Broadway
New York, New York 10019

The Alfred A. Knopf edition contains the following Library of Congress
Cataloging in Publication Data:

Schell, Jonathan. [*date*]
  The abolition.

  Includes index. 1. Atomic weapons and disarmament. 2. Deterrence
(Strategy) I. Title.
JX1974.7.S2194   1984   327.1'74   83-49355

First Avon Printing, May 1986

*I dedicate this book
with love to William Shawn.*

CONTENTS

I.

DEFINING THE GREAT PREDICAMENT

IN A SPEECH given in Hiroshima in February of 1981, Pope John Paul II said, "In the past, it was possible to destroy a village, a town, a region, even a country. Now it is the whole planet that has come under threat. This fact should fully compel everyone to face a basic moral consideration: from now on, it is only through a conscious choice and then deliberate policy that humanity can survive." The Pope's deceptively simple statement contains an invaluable anatomy of the challenge that the invention of nuclear weapons has placed before mankind. In the distinguishing between "a conscious choice" and "deliberate policy," he defines two stages—one individual and spiritual, the other public and political—that we must pass through if we are to resolve the nuclear predicament. Because by building large nuclear arsenals we threaten to extinguish ourselves as a species, each of us is called on to do something that no member of any generation before ours has had to do: to assume responsibility for the continuation of our kind—to *choose* human survival. There is nothing perfunctory or easy about making this choice. For example, it is wholly inadequate for us to remind ourselves that "nuclear war is horrible," and to assure ourselves that we are not "for" extinguishing mankind. The potential extermination of the human species by nuclear arms presents, like every monumental crime—Hitler's genocidal attack on the Jewish people being the most monstrous in memory—a challenge to the human spirit, and not one that we can be at all sure in advance that we are up to meeting. But even among monumental crimes the extermination of the species is unique. For the risk of extinction is not just one more item on the agenda of issues that faces us. Embracing, as it does, the life and death of every human being on earth and every future human being, it embraces and transcends all other issues. It is the ground in which they and every issue that might arise in the future have their significance and their being. But even to say that it is a life-and-death matter does not go far enough, because while the individual person may choose to give his life for causes that he considers to be greater and more important than his own life, including the cause of saving the lives of others, the extinction of mankind would destroy not only every person's life but also every larger cause, including the lives of all others, for which a person might be willing to give up his life. Extinction therefore threatens not so much each person's life (which is threatened at the same time by many other things, and will one day end anyway) as the *meaning* of our lives. It threatens life with meaninglessness as individual death never can. In doing so, it not only encompasses all human life but reaches deep into each life, requiring each of us to make this business his own. Sometimes it is suggested that it is ignoble to give the highest priority to our effort to save mankind from destruction, because in doing so we supposedly place our animal wish to stay alive above our higher, more specifically human obligation to live a morally decent life. But just the opposite is the case. It is precisely all those things *for which* people have throughout history been willing to sacrifice their lives that we have, indecently, now placed, in their entirety, at risk. And it is our desire to save those things—not merely the desire to save our own necks—which moves us to choose to save our species. It is also sometimes suggested that fear will inspire us to combat the nuclear peril, but that reasonable-sounding idea seems to me equally mistaken. Fear, a more or less reflexive response that we share with other species, drives each of us, as an individual, to save himself in the face of danger. Fear cannot distinguish between a fire in one's own house and a nuclear holocaust—between one's own death and the end of the world—and is therefore useless even to begin to suggest to us the meaning of the nuclear peril. Its meaning can be grasped only to the extent that we feel the precise opposite of fear, which is a sense of responsibility, or devotion, or love, for other people, including those who have not yet been born. In Germany, the peace movement has inverted the traditional Biblical admonition "Fear not" to say "You must fear." But the original version was the right one, for nuclear matters as for others. Fear isolates. Love connects. Only insofar as the latter is strong in us are we likely to find the resolve to prevent our extinction.

The conscious choice to take responsibility for the continuation of human life is further complicated and confused by the fact, which also is peculiar to the nuclear peril, that we are able to respond to it only before it happens. Since after extinction no one will be present to take responsibility, we have to take full responsibility now. It follows that we incur the full burden of guilt for extinguishing our species merely by preparing to do the deed, even without actually pushing the button. Sometimes it is suggested that while it would be a crime to extinguish mankind we are blameless if we intend—and threaten—to do so, provided that some laudable goal is being served by the threat. But if we absolve ourselves of responsibility for the intent, then we in effect evade responsibility altogether, since we can hardly assume responsibility after we are all dead. Therefore, insofar as we are going to take any responsibility whatever, we must in fact take it for the intent alone. To combine strategic with Christian terminology, we must adopt a policy of preemptive repentance. We must repent the crime before we commit it, and in that repentance find the will not to commit it. This displacement of repentance from the aftermath of the crime to the time preceding it would be, to paraphrase William James, the moral equivalent of deterrence. The only difference between it and the strategic sort is that whereas in strategic deterrence we are deterred by what the enemy may do to us, in moral deterrence we are deterred by what we may do to him—and to countless innocents, including all potential future generations of human beings. Or, to put it simply, we are not only fearful at the thought of suffering a nuclear holocaust but repelled by the thought of perpetrating one. Still, it would be misleading, perhaps, to try to distinguish too sharply between our fearful, selfish impulses and our altruistic, selfless ones. The holocaust itself will make no such distinctions. The fallout will fall on the just and the unjust alike. After the Cuban missile crisis, Premier Nikita Khrushchev remarked that the smell of burning flesh was in the air. But, in truth, that smell is never far from our nostrils now. The world's nuclear arsenals threaten to annihilate everyone in response to a transgression or mistake by any one party. That is how the doctrine of deterrence is designed. In consenting to live under it, we bear responsibility not only for the lives of the people whom "we" may kill but also for the lives of those whom "they" would kill; namely, our families, our friends, and our other fellow-citizens. Through the balance of terror, we all come to hold a dagger to the hearts of those nearest and dearest to us as well as to threaten those far away, down to the uttermost generations of human beings. The parent threatens the child, the lover the lover, the friend the friend, the citizen the citizen. Our acceptance of nuclear weapons is in that sense a default of parenthood, of love, of friendship, of citizenship, in which we all, like hijackers of airplanes, take one another hostage and threaten to kill one another. In acquiescing in the balance of terror, we become irresponsible parents, coldhearted lovers, faithless friends, and apathetic citizens. And in making a "conscious choice" to lift the nuclear peril we resolve to escape this pervasive corruption of our lives. We resolve to clear the air of the smell of burning flesh.

In making the choice, however, one decides nothing about the *means* of attaining the goal. That task is left

to the second stage: framing the "deliberate policy."
In fact, one has not even determined whether the goal
of bringing the species to safety is attainable. If it is not,
then our situation is tragic in the full sense of the word.
Then our species, while willing to live, would be fated
to die. And, indeed, there are many distinguished observers today who, while they do not write off the human species, believe that its safety cannot be very much
improved. In particular, they rule out the abolition of
nuclear weapons as impossible. For example, a *New
York Times* editorial critical of the recent pastoral letter
of the National Conference of Catholic Bishops on war
and peace, in which the bishops advocated the eventual
abolition of nuclear weapons, stated, "Fundamentally,
the American bishops' approach falters on the assumption that the nuclear dilemma can eventually be resolved by eliminating rather than controlling nuclear
weapons. But there is no known way to get rid of The
Bomb, no way to guard against all possible production
or concealments of warheads." And in *Living with Nuclear Weapons,* a book written at the request of Derek
Bok, the president of Harvard, by five professors and a
graduate student associated with Harvard—Albert
Carnesale, Paul Doty, Stanley Hoffmann, Samuel P.
Huntington, Joseph S. Nye, Jr., and Scott D. Sagan,
and published in 1982—it is stated that a world without
nuclear weapons is "a fictional utopia," and "humanity has no alternative but to hold this threat at bay and
to learn to live with politics, to live in the world we
know: a world of nuclear weapons, international rivalries, recurring conflicts, and at least some risk of nuclear crisis." In the closing paragraph of the Harvard
book, there is a memorable sentence, which the authors

apparently thought important enough to make use of for their title. It reads, ''Living with nuclear weapons is our only hope.'' This sentence could be engraved on our currency, alongside ''In God we trust,'' or perhaps replacing it, for it reflects accurately the faith of our time. We truly not only ''live with'' nuclear weapons but place our hope for the future in them. And now some of us have apparently arrived at a point at which we profess to have lost all hope without them. Yet if a nuclear-free world is really ''a fictional utopia,'' and if there is really ''no known way to get rid of The Bomb''—not even ''eventually''—then one must wonder what hope there is for mankind. Given the incurable fallibility of men and machines, doesn't it follow that sooner or later the bomb will get rid of us?

In the last few years, much of the public, having very largely ignored the nuclear peril for almost four decades, has been discovering a different faith. To express it in the Pope's terms, these people have been making their conscious choice: they have been choosing human survival. This long-delayed but deep and powerful public response is, like the predicament it addresses, a unique phenomenon, and familiar terms have to be stretched or altered to describe it, or even to name it. For example, it is both more and less than a ''peace movement''—the usual, and probably inescapable, term for it. It is more because the word ''movement'' suggests something of a political character, whereas this response was born and has gathered strength outside politics. It has begun as a pre-political stocktaking, in which people have been reexamining life itself, and every activity in life, in the light of the present peril to all life. This psychological and spiritual process, which is the very substance of the conscious choice, might be described as an awakening rather than a movement. The response is less than a traditional movement for much the same reason: though it stands poised at the edge of the political arena, and has already intervened, or tried to intervene, in certain decisions (the deployment of the new American missiles in Europe, for example), it has yet to find full political expression. That is, it has decided that it wants man to survive, but it has not (as its critics are quick to point out) settled on a ''deliberate policy'' for reaching its goal. Thus, it might be described as an awakening seeking to become a movement. This awakening is new, and its extent and its consequences are still uncertain, but it promises to be one of those great changes of heart in mankind—such as the awakening to the evil of slavery in the nineteenth century—that alter the psychological and spiritual map of the world, and, first acting outside politics, sweep into it with decisive effect. If politics is the art of the possible, then deep changes in opinion of this kind extend the boundaries of what the possible includes. (The political process in a democracy is broader than is sometimes supposed. When politicians speak of what is ''possible'' or ''impossible,'' they are often referring to nothing more than what is or is not acceptable to current public opinion. What they often really mean when they say that something is ''impossible'' is that they cannot win the next election if they advocate it. But if public opinion changes, then their opinion changes, too, and all of a sudden yesterday's impossible thing is possible.)

Just what may have triggered the new movement is a matter for speculation, but several circumstances and events are usually mentioned. They include the large buildup of nuclear arms by the Soviet Union in the last two decades, which has brought it up to the level of nuclear parity with the United States; the breakdown of the Strategic Arms Limitation Talks and the stalemate of the Strategic Arms Reduction Talks that succeeded them; the collapse of a mood of "détente" between the United States and the Soviet Union; the growing deployment by both the Soviet Union and the United States of missiles with the power to achieve a first strike against at least some missiles of the other side; the decision by the North Atlantic Treaty Organization to deploy intermediate-range nuclear missiles in Europe; and many provocative or ignorant-seeming statements regarding nuclear arms by officials of the Reagan Administration—statements such as one by T. K. Jones, the Deputy Under-Secretary of Defense for Research and Engineering, Strategic and Theatre Nuclear Forces, that "if there are enough shovels to go around, everybody's going to make it" through a nuclear holocaust, and, most important, the statement, in a top-secret Department of Defense planning document obtained by the *Times,* that the United States not only is planning for "prolonged" nuclear war but has as its aim to "prevail" in it—in plain language, to win it. But standing in the background of all these circumstances and events, I believe, is a development so simple and elementary that it is often overlooked. It is the fact that the doomsday machine—that immense collaborative undertaking of the United States and the Soviet Union, with minor assistance from other countries—has, over the last thirty-nine years, been assembled, with the finishing touches perhaps having been put on by the Soviet buildup. What was once merely a phrase in books is now actuality. And the real doomsday machine, lowering over the world, looks, feels, and is different in innumerable ways from the theoretical article. Of course, the doomsday machine didn't spring into existence all at once. The superpowers held no unveiling ceremony to announce to mankind that the preparations for the annihilation of the human species were now complete. Yet when people turned their attention to the nuclear peril they tended to see it all at once, with astonishment and horror, as though they had suddenly turned around and found themselves looking at a ferocious beast in the room with them. But looking at the nuclear peril was unlike any other looking. Because people were looking at things that they already in a sense knew about (the existence of nuclear arms had never been a secret), and not at some facts that had just been brought to light by reporters, it was a kind of looking within—a kind of introspection. And because these things that everyone already knew about were sickening and almost unbelievable, and because each person doing the looking was himself both implicated in and condemned by the evil, this looking within was anguishing. It seems not to be given to human beings to hold great horrors unremittingly before their mind's eye, and particularly not when the beholder is himself the potential perpetrator of the horror. We falter. We need respite. We forget. Then perhaps we look again. Alertness and stupor alternate. And we seem to lack any way of picturing extinction. The recent television film *The Day After* performed a public service by portraying Kansas after a nuclear attack. But no film can ever show the full consequences of a holocaust. It would have to display nothingness on the screen, and last forever. Even to try to understand the notion of extinction requires both intellectual and emotional effort. The boundlessness, the invisibility, and the emptiness of extinction are confounding. Extinction lacks the intricacy and detail that would permit our intellects to take hold of it—to analyze, to draw distinctions, to judge. Yet it is important to try to achieve an intellectual understanding of it, if only because by holding that in our mind we can sustain our effort and maintain our resolve without being dependent on the uncertainties of emotion. And, of course, as we strive, daily life in all its profusion goes on making its claims, introducing an at times comical disproportion in our lives between the immensity of our thoughts about the life and death of man and the smallness of our preoccupations with a particular personal quarrel, or meal, or financial worry, that may be absorbing us at a given moment. Weighing these incommensurables—deciding, for example, how much effort to expend to save the human species for all time as against how much to expend on, say, buying a sofa—is itself a considerable feat of balance and judgment.

Looking within themselves at the nuclear peril prepared people for action, and also was in itself a kind of action, albeit action taken within the privacy of each person's soul. Because this preparatory action—this coming to grips as a human being with the altered human situation—was not yet a political action, and prescribed no political course, it seemed to some as if it were nothing. That may be one reason the public awakening caught so many politicians and so much of the press by surprise: it had come about in domains of existence—the moral and spiritual—in which they ordinarily take little professional interest. That may also be the reason that, insofar as the movement has had leaders (a peculiar characteristic of it, apparently related to its grass-roots origin, has been its lack of conspicuous political leadership), they have tended to be doctors, including psychiatrists, and clergymen—people ordinarily concerned not with politics but with disturbances in the body, the psyche, and the soul. The new disturbances were, in fact, seismic. Suddenly, people were awash in fathomless questions of human existence. How did it happen, people started to ask themselves, that we have become the underwriters of the slaughter of billions of innocent people? Can such slaughter ever be justified? How? What is the meaning of human life on earth? What would its extermination mean? What does it mean about us that we have built the equipment with which to carry out that extermination, and are apparently prepared to perform the act? What does it mean that we—one link in the chain of the generations—are prepared to cut the chain, and set adrift in darkness all the future generations of human beings? What is our responsibility to these unborn people, and how can we fulfill it?

These questions are no newer than the technical invention that propelled them into the thick of history: they were raised in 1945, in the stunned aftermath of the Hiroshima bombing. Yet before long they receded from people's thoughts, as though they were too shocking for people to take to heart on such short notice. We who are alive today, however, thirty-nine years into the nuclear world, stand on different historical ground. Some of us have moved through the years of our lives in the shadow of peril—have grown up, come of age, married, had children, worked, and approached death in the knowledge that before long all mankind may die. In one sense, our experience of the peril is oblique (no nuclear blast has been directed against human beings since Nagasaki), but in another sense it is fundamental, since if mankind destroys itself with nuclear weapons no one will experience our disappearance after the fact, and our experience of that fate now, before it happens, is all the experience of it that anyone will ever get. It *is* the experience of extinction. What we feel, therefore, is not so much fear of a future event, such as we feel when we realize that one day something terrible may happen to us, as it is disgust at the debasement of life right now because it is threatened by and threatens the extinction of man.

To make the choice is essential, for without it we are simply becalmed—as we were until very recently. If the inner landscape of our souls does not change, the outer landscape of the world will not change, either. And once the choice has been made it must, like every profound moral and spiritual decision, be continually refreshed and renewed. Since the beginning of history, human beings have stood in wonder at the blessing of life within them and around them. But now, for the first time, that wonder implies a political obligation. Every beautiful morning, every note of song, every infant's smile must propel us into action. Making and sustaining the conscious choice is a labor that has an integrity of its own, independent of what we may propose to do about the nuclear predicament. Just as in medicine the diagnosis precedes the prescription, and lays the basis for it, the conscious choice must precede the deliberate policy.

But then we must frame the deliberate policy. If we fail, the cost to us—even if it happens that we do not stumble into oblivion—is that our wonder at life and our joy in it will be progressively diminished and corrupted. The choice must be made so that the policy can follow; but if the policy does not follow—if, instead, we sink back into stupefaction and complacency—the choice itself will be undone. Worse, it will, in effect, be reversed: by default, we will have chosen annihilation. In these pages, I propose to address the question of deliberate policy—specifically, the question of how we might abolish nuclear arms—but first, as a way of framing the policy question, I would like, by sketching out the chief features of our predicament (including, briefly, the facts that underlie the peril itself, some of which have come to light only recently), and by discussing some of the responses to the predicament over the years, to describe the elements of what appears to be a historic impasse, in which the world has now been stuck for almost four decades.

As citizens, we would like to know what the consequences of a nuclear holocaust at various levels of nuclear armament would be. We would like to know how many weapons kill how many people; how many weapons would be necessary to annihilate a particular country (our own, for example); and how many would be necessary to destroy our whole species. In search of answers to these questions, we naturally turn to scientists. But when we do we find that they can offer us only a portion of the information that either they or we need in order to make a firm judgment. That this should be so is not the fault of today's scientists, who have made impressive strides in understanding the natural world.

Rather, it is due to humanity's still having only a rudimentary over-all comprehension of the living systems whose destruction or mutilation is in question; namely, human societies, ecosystems, and, ultimately, the earth itself—which is to say life itself, insofar as it has been given to human beings to know life. What is known about the earth is awesome—as readers of the September, 1983, issue of *Scientific American,* for example, which takes the workings of the earth as its subject, can appreciate. Yet what remains unknown is more awesome still. What is known seems towering until one looks at how much there remains to find out, and then it seems minuscule.

The crucial role of uncertainty in assessing the consequences of a nuclear holocaust needs some emphasis, because it is often overlooked or misunderstood by people who, for understandable reasons, would like simple and clear factual answers. The scientists can speak with great confidence about the properties of the weapons, which they invented and have observed in tests. But as soon as they begin to speak about the effects of those weapons on the surrounding world uncertainty sets in. For instance, it is known that land-surface nuclear explosions would create large amounts of radioactive fallout. Yet there has never been a true land-surface explosion of a bomb with a yield of more than one kiloton. The farther we get from the simple, immediate effects of the weapons—the initial nuclear radiation, the electromagnetic pulse, the thermal pulse, the blast wave, the local fallout—the more speculative our knowledge becomes. Maximum uncertainty is reached when we get to the question of extinction. Nuclear weapons threaten our species with extinction not because every last person on earth would be blown up or irradiated in a nuclear holocaust (something that could conceivably come close to happening in the targeted nations, though not in all the nations of the earth) but because a holocaust might so drastically alter the ecosphere that the earth would become uninhabitable by human beings.

The story of the advances that have been made in our understanding of the effects of a holocaust implies the unfinished state of our present knowledge of the total effects. That story has been one of continual surprises. The first surprise was the atomic bomb itself, which not ten years before its invention had been declared by many eminent scientists to be an unlikelihood bordering on an impossibility. Even Albert Einstein is reported to have remarked in 1935 that to split the atom would be akin to shooting birds in the dark in a country where there were few birds. Perhaps the next surprise, which came as a result of atmospheric testing, was the huge amount and range of radioactive fallout; its extent was unsuspected until it began falling on Pacific islanders and American servicemen after the American test on Bikini Atoll, in 1954. A further surprise that came during testing was the electromagnetic pulse—a gigantic surge of electricity that is generated by gamma radiation acting on air. The electromagnetic pulse of just one big nuclear bomb, if it is detonated high above the United States, may, it is now believed, damage solid-state electrical circuits throughout the continental United States and in parts of Canada and Mexico. A more recent surprise was the discovery, made in the early 1970's, of a danger to the ozone layer—one that in terms of global damage could be the most serious of the dangers that had been discovered up to that time. A report by the National Academy of Sciences in 1975 on *Long-Term Worldwide Effects of Multiple Nuclear-Weapons Detonations* found that after a holocaust in which ten thousand megatons were detonated ozone reduction might be as high as seventy per cent in the Northern Hemisphere (where all the detonations were assumed to have occurred) and forty per cent in the Southern Hemisphere. The formation of an ozone layer is believed to have been a precondition for the emergence of multicellular life, and of life on land, because ozone blocks out wavelengths of ultraviolet light that are harmful to many forms of life, and while reductions in the ozone of the magnitudes mentioned in the report would not eliminate all organisms with more than one cell or drive life back into the sea they could pervasively harm both plant and animal life, and their ultimate consequences for the earth's varied ecosystems are unforeseeable. Weighing these effects of a nuclear holocaust, scientists gave us warning that extinction was a possibility. For example, in March of 1982, in support of a proposal for joint hearings by the House Foreign Affairs Committee and the Senate Foreign Relations Committee on the effects of a holocaust, a number of scientists made statements on the subject. Marvin Goldberger, the president of the California Institute of Technology, said, "Full-scale war would eliminate humanity to all intents and purposes. Survival itself would be questionable." Paul Marks, the president of the Memorial Sloan-Kettering Cancer Center, said, "Nuclear war would wipe out the [human] race where the war was fought, and it could exterminate the entire race. It would make half the world uninhabitable. I'm not sure of the effect on the other half. It would probably make it un-inhabitable, too.'' Other scientists who were quoted in favor of the proposal placed greater stress on the chances for survival. For example, Lewis Thomas, president emeritus of Sloan-Kettering, said, ''Nuclear war would almost surely destroy human society. We would lose all of what we call culture. U.S.-U.S.S.R. conflict would eliminate the Northern Hemisphere for all practical purposes. The Southern Hemisphere might survive. I doubt that all humans would be extermi-nated.'' But whether they were pessimistic or optimis-tic about the chances for human survival the scientists surrounded their opinions with appropriate expressions of doubt, saying that extinction was ''possible,'' or that the Southern Hemisphere ''might'' survive. Their common ground was uncertainty.

The wisdom of these scientists' reluctance to make final judgments became abundantly clear late last year, when, at a conference in Washington called ''The World After Nuclear War,'' another group of eminent scientists revealed the latest surprise in the unfolding and obviously unfinished story of the effects of a nu-clear holocaust. They had concluded that in a holocaust soil and dust from the explosions and smoke from fires set by the explosions would create a dark cloud over the earth which would largely block out sunlight, turning day into twilight or night, and drastically lowering the temperature, to create a ''nuclear winter.'' The way in which this discovery was made is instructive of the un-expected ways in which science moves forward. One important new element in the discovery was space travel. In 1971, Mariner 9—the first space craft to go into orbit around another planet—began to circle Mars.

Aboard was an infrared interferometric spectrometer—an instrument that could measure temperatures on the surface of Mars and at various heights in the atmosphere above it. As it happened, Mars was enveloped in a global dust storm when Mariner 9 arrived. The spectrometer showed that the atmosphere of Mars was considerably warmer than it usually was, and the surface considerably cooler: the dust in the atmosphere was absorbing sunlight, thus warming the atmosphere, and was blocking it from reaching the surface, thus cooling the surface. A group of scientists concerned with parallels between the earth and other planets—Richard Turco, an atmospheric physicist in Marina del Rey, California; Owen Toon, Thomas Ackerman, and James Pollack, all from the National Aeronautics and Space Administration's Ames Research Center; and Carl Sagan, the director of the Laboratory for Planetary Studies at Cornell—set about applying these findings to terrestrial questions. Their interest was spurred by a recently advanced hypothesis that the extinction of the dinosaurs at the end of Cretaceous period, sixty-five million years ago, might have resulted from a drop in light and temperature brought about when an asteroid crashed into the earth, lofting a cover of dust into the terrestrial atmosphere.

Meanwhile, two other scientists—Paul Crutzen, of the Max Planck Institute for Chemistry, in Mainz, Germany, and John Birks, of the University of Colorado—had calculated that smoke generated by the fires that would be started by nuclear explosions would greatly decrease the sunlight reaching the earth. (In fact, the smoke would be more important than the dust in blocking sunlight.) The earth—its cities and its forests in par-

ticular—is like a well-laid fire. If you light it with
enough nuclear matches, it will burn, and as it burns it
will fill the atmosphere with smoke and plunge much of
the world into a frigid darkness for several months.
These findings, which were published in 1982, and the
findings from Mars led Turco and his colleagues to conduct a study that they eventually called *Nuclear Winter:
Global Consequences of Multiple Nuclear Explosions*.
They concluded that within two weeks after a holocaust
in which five thousand megatons were used had occurred in the Northern Hemisphere the cloud of smoke
would circle the hemisphere. A deep gloom would have
gathered, and land temperatures would be falling. Also,
a toxic smog, loaded with hydrogen cyanide and other
debris of the burned cities, could cover the hemisphere.
A few weeks later, the cloud would penetrate the Southern Hemisphere, and land temperatures there would
also begin to fall. After a holocaust in which ten thousand megatons were used (the study estimated this to be
about three-quarters of what is available in present strategic arsenals, whose exact megatonnage is unknown),
temperatures at the center of continents in the Northern
Hemisphere could sink as low as twenty-three degrees
below zero Fahrenheit, even in summer. Near coast-
lines, the temperatures would be more moderate, because of the warming influence of the sea, but violent,
monsoon-like storms cause by the difference between
inland and ocean temperatures could be expected. After
a period lasting from several months to a year, the cloud
would have largely dissipated, and sunlight, now unfortunately including the biologically harmful ultraviolet light let in by the ozone loss, would reach the
surface again. In the Southern Hemisphere, the drops

in temperature and the other effects would be less severe. One of the most surprising findings of the study was that as little as a hundred megatons—less than one per cent of the world's arsenals—could, if it were to be targeted on urban centers, trigger a less severe but still catastrophic nuclear winter, in which temperatures could drop more than fifty degrees Fahrenheit. Thus, there appears to be a threshold—determined by the number of explosions it would take to set a significant number of cities on fire—above which the major features of this climatic catastrophe would occur.

The human and biological consequences of the nuclear winter literally defy representation. Some are gross and obvious. People would freeze. They would find it difficult to see what they were doing. Crops wouldn't grow, so they would starve. Other animals would freeze and starve. If the holocaust occurred during the growing season, then "virtually all land plants in the Northern Hemisphere would be damaged or killed," in the words of Paul Ehrlich, professor of biological sciences at Stanford University, who presented a report to the conference on the biological consequences of the nuclear winter. "In the oceans, the darkness would inhibit photosynthesis in the tiny green plants (algae) that form the base of all significant marine food chains," Ehrlich said. "Tropical forests could largely disappear." The combined consequences of the nuclear winter, coming on top of the other effects, which in themselves could kill or wound billions of people and would shatter the elementary equipment of civilization by which modern man survives, lie far beyond our power of prediction, but they could, in words of Ehrlich's that, in the light of the new discoveries, add urgency to the words of warning we had already had from other scientists, ''entrain the extinction of humanity.''

The question of whether nuclear weapons might extinguish mankind first came up in the 1940s, in a context slightly different from the present one. As the team of scientists at Los Alamos was preparing for the detonation of the first bomb, it occurred to someone that the heat of the explosion might be so great that it would ignite the earth's atmosphere and burn it up, ending not only human life but all life on earth. Robert Oppenheimer, the director of the project, took the danger seriously enough to ask a group of scientists on the team to figure out whether or not this would happen. The group found not only that the temperature of the bomb would be insufficient to set the atmosphere on fire but that the temperature needed to do that was so high that it could never be reached by any nuclear explosion. Armed with this assurance, the Los Alamos team went ahead and set off the bomb. (In social, if not in scientific, terms the group's calculation may be described as the most important ever made by scientists.) One wonders whether the team would have done so if the group had come back with a less reassuring answer—if, for example, it had said that there was a one-in-a-hundred chance that the bomb would set the atmosphere on fire. Whatever the team might have done then, now that more than fifty thousand nuclear weapons stand ready to be detonated in the world's arsenals no such assurance regarding the survival of our species in the event of a holocaust is, or can be, forthcoming from responsible scientists. The physicist Theodore Taylor has said, ''The consequences of nuclear war are unpredictable. The extinction of the species forever cannot be ruled out by any process of scientific investigation.'' We will gain more knowledge. (Already, a Russian scientist at the ''World After Nuclear War'' conference has suggested that the warming of the upper atmosphere by the smoke and soot from a holocaust will melt glaciers and snows in high mountain ranges, creating floods ''of continental magnitude.'') But our knowledge will never be complete. To accept uncertainty is essential in facing the nuclear peril honestly, and to learn to make judgments, and to act on them, in the midst of uncertainty is the beginning of wisdom in dealing with the nuclear predicament. It is especially important to avoid all false assurances and pseudo certainty. These, unfortunately, are rife, and include not only baseless, dogmatic judgments about the ultimate effects of a holocaust but also a large array of doubtful ''strategic'' predictions concerning precisely what moves and countermoves might be made in a holocaust.

Once the citizen has gone to the scientists and received the information that they have available, he must, without further professional help, take counsel with himself. The scientists can tell what they know; they can tell what they suspect; and they can guess with the rest of us about how much there may still be to find out. In putting his questions to the scientists, the citizen has already in a way asked them to venture beyond the proper limits of their disciplines, for he has asked them not for the proved results of experimentation but for speculation that is unprovable, unless we blow up the earth in search of answers. Because of the importance of the issue, the scientists oblige us with their best answers while candidly confessing the uncertainty and incompleteness of their findings. It would obviously be a mistake for the citizen to do what the scientists have warned against, and treat educated speculation as hard, scientific fact. The most valuable thing that the citizen carries away from the scientists' report, I suggest, is not any particular estimate—the percentage of ozone reduction, for example, or the level of temperature drop in the nuclear winter—for most of these estimates have been revised many times in the past and may be revised again in the future, and are, in any case, almost certainly an incomplete catalogue of effects. It is, rather, a broad sense of the power of a nuclear holocaust to throw the ecosphere as a whole into catastrophic disorder.

As the citizen takes stock of the perils, at least two considerations that lie outside the range of scientific evidence must come into play. The first is that effects of a nuclear holocaust will not fail to occur merely because they haven't been predicted. It may be that, say, only fifty per cent of them have been discovered, but a hundred per cent of them will occur. Unless—like the advocates of Newtonian physics at the end of the nineteenth century, who thought that with the scientific achievements of their time the edifice of physics had essentially been completed—we have the arrogance to believe that our present knowledge of the earth is perfect, we have no choice but to assume that the list of surprises is not complete. It should help us to preserve modesty in making judgments about the effects of a nuclear holocaust to recall that if we had sought in, say, 1950 to make a final judgement about those effects we would have seriously underestimated or left entirely out of account what are perhaps the three most important global effects that have been discovered so far: the extent of fallout; ozone loss; and the nuclear winter. The second consideration is that from a human point of view our extinction is an unlimited consequence. It would not only put an end to the living generations but foreclose all future generations, down to the end of time. It would mark the defeat of all human strivings, all human hopes, all human ideals, past and future. For now human beings, engaged, as always, in the ambitions and disputes of their particular place and time, can end the human story in all places for all time. The eternal has been placed at stake in the temporal realm, and the infinite has been delivered into the care of finite human beings. It is because of this special nature of the peril, I believe, that the very existence of uncertainty about whether or not a holocaust would extinguish our species should lead us to treat the issue morally and politically *as though* it were a certainty. That is, when we turn to the nuclear predicament we should muster all the commitment that loyalty to our species can inspire. In my book *The Fate of the Earth* (1982), I wrote a passage that emphasizes the importance of uncertainty, and I repeat it here to clarify the reason for treating the uncertainty *as though* it were certainty:

We know that a holocaust may not occur at all. If one does occur, the adversaries may not use all their weapons. If they do use all their weapons, the global effects, in the ozone and elsewhere, may be moderate. And if the effects are not moderate but extreme, the ecosphere may prove resilient enough to withstand them without breaking down catastrophically. These are all substantial reasons for supposing that mankind will not be extinguished in a nuclear holocaust, or even that extinction in a holocaust is unlikely, and they tend to calm our fear and to reduce our sense of urgency. Yet at the same time we are compelled to admit that there *may* be a holocaust, that the adversaries *may* use all their weapons, that the global effects, including effects of which we are as yet unaware, *may* be severe, that the ecosphere *may* suffer catastrophic breakdown, and that our species *may* be extinguished. We are left with uncertainty.

I concluded, "Once we learn that a holocaust *might* lead to extinction we have no right to gamble, because if we lose, the game will be over, and neither we nor anyone else will ever get another chance. Therefore, although, scientifically speaking, there is all the difference in the world between the mere possibility that a holocaust will bring about extinction and the certainty of it, morally they are the same, and we have no choice but to address the issue of nuclear weapons as though we knew for a certainty that their use would put an end to our species." It is in this spirit that I continue here to speak of nuclear weapons as an issue of life or death for mankind.

The totality of the peril (in the sense just defined) is, of course, the most important feature of the nuclear predicament. It must inevitably shape and color all our thinking on the subject, including our thinking on what we should do about the predicament. A second, less often mentioned feature, which is of importance to the policy question, is the abruptness with which the peril arrived. Great changes had occurred in the conditions of life before, but they had arrived gradually. The industrial revolution, for example, transformed the way people lived, but it was made up of innumerable technical innovations that were released into the world over centuries, so that people had time to make their adjustments. The industrial revolution would offer a closer analogy if all the inventions made between, say 1700 and 1945 had somehow arrived at once, in 1700. The nuclear predicament—the result of the invention of a *single* device—sprang into the world full-fledged, offering little time for reflection or adjustment. (There did remain the time required to build up the arsenals—a sort of grace period—but it was very short, and, in any case, has been squandered.) Slavery offers another analogy. It was there at the beginning of history, and it took mankind millennia to finally confront the practice and abolish it. But when nuclear weapons were invented a brand-new evil was suddenly created, as though slavery had been lowered into our midst in an instant. And we did not have the luxury of millennia in which to react. The peril was immediate, and called on us to act right away.

A third feature of the predicament, which is also of importance to the policy question, is the peril's apparent everlastingness. While nuclear weapons can, I believe, one day be eliminated, the knowledge of how to make them, which is rooted in our century's fundamental discoveries in physics, appears likely to be with us forever, and since that is so the possibility that nuclear arsenals will be rebuilt and used cannot be ruled out. We are not condemned to live always in a world armed with nuclear weapons, but we shall always live in a nuclear world. In that respect, nuclear energy is like a new sun that has risen over the earth—a sun that will beam its bleak light on human affairs as long as the sun in the sky will. We speak of "the nuclear age," but since, strictly speaking, that "age," like the period "after Christ," has no end in view, it would be more appropriate to speak, in the Latin phrase, of "a new order of the ages." But perhaps if we optimistically suppose that nuclear weapons (though not the knowledge of how to make them) will one day be abolished we can call the period up to then "the nuclear age"—and pray that it will be short.

As if it were not enough that the threat posed by the nuclear peril was unlimited in its scope, instantaneous in its appearance, and everlasting in its staying power, a fourth key feature of the predicament is that nuclear weapons immediately lodged themselves at the very heart of international decision-making, and so carried revolutionary global political implications. Given all the rest, it might seem that the revolutionary political implications would hardly need mention, but the fact is that one can imagine perils on an equal scale physically whose political solution would be relatively simple. For example, it was discovered some years ago that certain types of spray cans release gases which, like the products of nuclear explosions, can rise into the stratosphere, where they decompose, and that their components erode the ozone layer. Let us suppose that scientists had discovered (as in fact they have not) that at present levels of spray-can use the erosion of the ozone layer would go far enough to doom all land animals in ten years. We can have little doubt that the nations of the earth would quickly sign a treaty abolishing spray cans. Or let us suppose that scientists had discovered (as, again, they have not) that, beyond a certain threshold, the burning of fossil fuels would trigger a runaway ''greenhouse effect'' in the atmosphere, in which the temperature of the earth would rise to lethal levels. (Scientists suspect that a runaway greenhouse effect may be responsible for the seven-hundred-degree surface temperature of Venus. They also suspect that a greenhouse effect produced by the burning of fossil fuels will warm the earth by several degrees in the next hundred years.) Once again, it is hard to doubt that, despite the importance of fossil fuels, the nations of the earth would quickly sign a treaty bringing their use under control. For it would surely very soon become clear to people everywhere that they valued humanity more than they valued fossil fuels. Or if we imagine that one day we were attacked by creatures from space whose aim was to destroy mankind and take over the planet, it is again hard to doubt that the nations of the earth would unite to defend their planet. (The Soviet Union and the United States even managed to unite to defeat the earthly peril of Nazi Germany.) Yet when it comes to saving the earth from the peril of a nuclear holocaust the necessary agreements are not arrived at so easily— as the history of the last thirty-nine years attests. And for this failure there is a substantial cause that would not be a factor in any of the foregoing, imagined situations. The solution of each of those threats would require us to give something up—spray cans, fossil fuels, the immediate pursuit of earthly rivalries. But if we ask what it is that we would have to give up in order to resolve the nuclear predicament we find that it is nothing less than the whole present structure of international affairs. For the very first effect of the invention of nuclear weapons—which occurred even without their going off—was to fatally undermine the institution of war.

It may seem odd to speak of war, the nemesis of human institutions, as an institution itself, liable to change and decline like any other, yet we are now in a position to see that it has been just that: a particular kind of organization of human affairs, with a particular character, a particular technical foundation, and particular uses. Its preeminent use has been to serve as what has been called since Roman times "the final arbiter" of disputes among nations—as the world's means of last resort for getting things settled. But when nuclear weapons entered the arsenals of nations, war could no longer arbitrate anything, because the levels of force available would destroy every prize that a nation might want either to seize or to defend. Nations bent on achieving some aim by the use of force, whether the aim was their own survival or another country's subjugation, could not hope to succeed in a nuclear-armed world. To be sure, nuclear-armed nations could still attack one another (if they were foolish enough), but at the end of the road only their "mutual assured destruction" now awaited them. This would not be war—once defined as "the continuation of politics by other means"—but only suicide, which is the continuation of nothing.

It's worth noting that the point in the nuclear buildup at which mutual assured destruction became possible (and victory in war impossible) is different from the point at which extinction became possible. Perhaps because both results are absurd, the two are sometimes lumped together. The difference becomes obvious if we imagine that two small countries, each of which can be annihilated with just a few dozen nuclear weapons, are faced off against one another. Each would destroy the other long before the two together could extinguish the species. When the countries are large, however, the gap between mutual assured destruction and extinction is narrower, and the new conclusion that even "limited nuclear war" might trigger the nuclear winter narrows this gap still further. In a general holocaust, the mutual destruction of the belligerents would be only a minor absurdity within the major, unlimited absurdity of the end of humanity. Nevertheless, the potential for mutual assured destruction needs to be underscored, because it is precisely *this* minor absurd outcome—which does not depend on the presence of a peril of extinction—that spoils war as a rational instrument of national policy, and forces nations to look for a substitute. (The possibility of extinction, above and beyond mutual assured destruction, gives their search a transcendent importance.)

To avoid misunderstanding: When I say that war has been spoiled as a means of settling international disputes, I mean that it has been spoiled in those theatres of potential conflict in which the rivals are abundantly armed with nuclear weapons, as the United States and the Soviet Union are. In other theatres, in which one or both powers lack nuclear weapons, nations can and do go on fighting wars. To avoid further misunderstanding: What has been ruined is, precisely, war—no more and no less. Violence between nuclear-armed states is still possible on any scale, from terrorist acts right up to the end of the world, but none of this would, properly speaking, be war. For war is not just violence; it is violence shaped to achieve state ends. But all these ends would be unattainable by "war" as it exists today, for by the time anyone had "won" the "war" both sides would have been annihilated.

In sum, the underlying *human* question that the invention of nuclear weapons confronts us with is whether we will live or die as a species, but the underlying *political* question, which must be tackled before the human question can be favorably resolved, is how disputes among nations are to be handled in a world in which war has been spoiled as an instrument of state policy. Nuclear weapons are radical biologically and spiritually because they threaten our species with extinction, but they are radical politically because they have spoiled war. For traditionally the political character of our world has been determined in large part by the outcome of wars—by whether the Romans or the Carthaginians, Napoleon or Wellington, the Axis or the Allies, were victorious. At stake, therefore, *in addition* to the life or death of mankind, is everything that nations are and everything that they stand for, since it is through war that nations in the past have sought ultimately to protect their existence. How, we are now forced to ask, are we to defend the things that we believe in—or, on a more prosaic level, that we merely want? (For the United States, and for the Western alliance, the chief question of this sort is, perhaps, how we can protect our liberties and, by a reasonable extension, liberty in the world as a whole.) How are nations to respond to aggression? Or should there any longer even *be* nations, which, continuing their historical reliance on the resort to force in pursuit of their parochial interests, now menace the survival of all mankind? At issue is *who* is going to decide international disputes and *how*—and these are, of course, the fundamental issues of politics. Should nations decide through violence, as in the past? Should an international authority decide? Is there another way of deciding? No proposal that fails to give an answer to this underlying question can inspire confidence, and only a proposal that deals with it to the world's satisfaction seems likely to stand a chance of finally resolving the nuclear predicament.

There is a strong temptation to underestimate either the biological or the political dimension of the peril, because then the job of finding a solution is much simplified. For example, if we choose to disregard the radical nature of the political issue, then, responding without impediment to the totality and immediacy of the peril, we are free to imagine that we can ''ban'' nuclear weapons without further ado—without, that is, having to account for how, politically, a nuclear-free world would work, what would be likely to happen in it, and whether or not it would be likely to stay nuclear-free. On the other hand, if, duly impressed by the intractability of the political challenge, we choose instead to play down the physical immediacy and totality of the peril, we may complacently and unconscionably leave our species at risk of annihilation. Such, I believe, is our present condition.

The difficulty of taking all the features of the nuclear predicament into account was made clear in the first attempts to discover solutions. Sheer thought, of course, was able to see its way to a solution quite easily. The steps in the reasoning were simple ones. If war now meant nuclear war—and no one could doubt that it did—and nuclear war meant, at best, the mutual assured destruction of the belligerents and, at worst, human extinction, then war no longer made any sense and would have to be given up. But if war was give up, then some other means would have to be found to resolve the disputes that war had always resolved. A means was not hard to find—at least, on the purely intellectual plane. It was government—world government. The rule of law would supplant the rule of force, and what had once been decided by violence would now be decided by courts, parliaments, and all the other institutions of civil society. In the early days of the nuclear age, many people, including, notably, many scientists, were swayed by this compelling logic, and soon set to work to bring a world government into existence. Preeminent among them, perhaps, was Albert Einstein, who, at the beginning of the century, had first revealed that energy and matter are the same. As early as September 29, 1945— less than two months after the bomb was dropped on Hiroshima, on August 6—he wrote:

The pathetic attempts made by governments to achieve what they consider to be international security have not the slightest effect on the present political structure of the world, nor is it recognized that the real cause of international conflicts is due to the existence of competing sovereign nations. Neither governments nor people seem to have learned anything from the experiences of the past and appear to be unable or unwilling to think the problem through. The conditions existing in the world today force the individual states, out of fear for their own security, to commit acts which inevitably produce war.

At the present high level of industrialization and economic interdependence, it is unthinkable that we can achieve peace without a genuine supranational organization to govern international relations.

At about the same time, Einstein was one of the signatories of a letter, published in the *New York Times*, that said, in part:

We have learned, and paid an awful price to learn, that living and working together can be done in one way only—under law. There is no truer and simpler idea in the world today. Unless it prevails, and unless by common struggle we are capable of new ways of thinking, mankind is doomed.

And in June of 1946 he told an interviewer:

Our defense is not in armaments, nor in science, nor in going underground. Our defense is in law and order.

Einstein knew very well that the political climate of his time was hostile to his proposal, and he knew that many people regarded it as, in his words, "illusory, even absurd." Nevertheless, in a reply to critics, he asked:

Is it really a sign of unpardonable naiveté to suggest that those in power decide among themselves that future conflicts must be settled by constitutional means rather than by the senseless sacrifice of great numbers of human lives? Once such a firm decision has been reached, nothing will be "impossible." . . .

A "sophisticated" person might well comment: We have been working toward the same goal by means of small, patient steps, which, in view of human psychology, is the only possible method. But I, the so-called "idealist," regard this attitude as a fatal illusion. There is no *gradual* way to secure peace. As long as nations have no real security against aggression, they will, inevitably, continue to prepare for war. And, as history has proven conclusively, preparation for war always leads to actual war. When the North American Colonies united and created a central government in Washington, it came about not through a slow process but through a resolute and creative act.

In interviews, articles, letters, and public statements, Einstein, continuing to state his case with his customary clarity, modesty, simplicity, and passion, advocated this position until the end of his life, in April, 1955.

Einstein's view that the nuclear predicament could be resolved and mankind saved only if the world renounced force and adopted peaceful political means for the settlement of its disputes possessed a straightforward logic that no one ever refuted and that was apparently irrefutable. (His view that the only such means possible was world government was more debatable.) But what logic called for and what the world was prepared to accept were two different things. Einstein set out to change minds. He knew, as few other men did, what the measure of the peril was, and he worked tirelessly to impart that knowledge to others. As a scientist, he was used to thinking a problem through to its end, and he thought the political implications of the nuclear predicament through to their end, too. He placed his faith in reason—in people's ability to learn, and to act on what they have learned. He had changed the world through scientific thought, and now he wanted to change it further through political thought. In that sense, world government was a scientists' *sort* of idea. Using reason, scientists analyzed the problem, came up with a formula that would solve it, and then invited the world to apply that formula. Einstein wrote, "Just as we have changed our thinking in the world of pure science to embrace newer and more useful concepts, so we must now change our thinking in the world of politics and law. It is too late to make mistakes." And, even more simply, "Past thinking and methods did not succeed in preventing world wars. Future thinking *must* prevent wars." But politics was different from science, and thinking turned out not to have the effectiveness in world affairs that it had had in the laboratory. In politics, the process was different and the tempo was different. Political ideas moved at a slower pace than scientific ones from one mind to the minds of many, and from the minds of many into action.

Certainly one cause of the world's apparent indifference to the nuclear peril, and of the short shrift it gave the idea of world government, was the peril's all-or-nothing character, which removed it from people's direct experience. Most evils arrive in the world a little bit at a time, so that in pushing people into action the bite of painful experience is added to the voice of pure reason. If a factory is polluting the water supply, for example, deadly poison doesn't suddenly start running from the tap; the pollution appears gradually, and people are driven to do something before a catastrophe occurs. But after Hiroshima and Nagasaki the nuclear peril turned out to leave the world physically untouched, and the field was left to "thinking" alone. There can be little doubt that if in the last thirty-nine years one Hiroshima-sized nuclear weapon had gone off each day in a city somewhere in the world (thus releasing, in all, only about one per cent of the explosive power of today's arsenals) Einstein's proposal, or something of an equally radical nature, would have found acceptance by now. As it was, the nuclear weapons fortunately stayed unexploded (while unfortunately multiplying in the world's arsenals), and people were not impelled to think or do very much about them.

The stronger reasons for the rejection of the sweeping changes that Einstein wanted, however, were unquestionably political. Arrayed against his argument was not so much counter-argument as brute fact—everything that comes under the heading of political "reality," which in the short run, at least, has a weight and an inertia that are independent of argument and the light of reason. On the immediate level, reality was two great powers—the United States and the Soviet Union—whose systems of government were wholly antithetical. While it was quite conceivable that these two powers could live together without war—that is, "coexist"—there seemed little or no possibility that they could fuse into a single government. Reality was, in addition, the countless unresolved struggles that went on, and go on, among the less powerful nations of the world, dividing Arab from Jew, Irishman from English, Turk from Greek, and so on. On the deepest level, however, reality was the entire political organization of the world. Standing in the way of Einstein's "thinking," that is, was nothing less than the world's political institutions as they had existed throughout history—the entire system of independent states, whose defense now threatened extinction. The invention of nuclear weapons brought basic physical and biological reality, now radically transformed by the revolution in scientific thought, into head-on collision with basic political reality, where no similar revolution appeared likely soon. And the collision was not just a clash of styles, or a failure of scientists and politicians to speak one another's language; it was objective and real. Science had moved with the speed of thought to alter physical reality and to give technical man the ability to place the whole world in peril of annihilation, but the political thinkers were powerless to perform a comparable miracle in political affairs. Political affairs, weighted with tradition and habit—in this case, a way of doing things which had lasted throughout history—moved with a ponderous gait of their own, and were not to be hurried. The nuclear predicament had emerged in an instant from the laboratory, but the resolution of the predicament could not emerge from any laboratory. It would have to be born in its own time, in the hearts of the billions of the earth's people.

The disparity between the swiftness of science in presenting the peril (a swiftness much accentuated, from the world's point of view, by the governmental secrecy out of which the bomb sprang) and the seemingly built-in slowness of the world's thinking and the world's institutions to adjust to it presented the world, in effect, with a monumental problem of timing. While the predicament might not be inherently beyond resolution, the mismatch between the immediacy of the peril and the magnitude of the psychological, spiritual, and political work required for mankind to make an adequate response—which might conceivably take generations—could in itself prove fatal. The proposal for world government therefore engendered as much discouragement as hope. Many people believed that a solution might lie there, but they could not see how to arrive at it soon enough to respond to the pressing emergency in which the species found itself. Nor did sovereignty show any signs of expiring on its own. If anything, it was tightening its hold—especially in the Third World, where patriotic feeling was showing itself to be an almost irresistible force, against which the great colonial empires of the West were proving powerless.

In those circumstances, it was anything abut surprising that a second school of thought about how to handle the nuclear predicament soon emerged—a school that was ready to accept the unwillingness of nations to surrender their sovereignty and enter into a world government. In 1946, in a book called *The Absolute Weapon*, by a group of academics at the Yale Institute of International Studies, there appeared two chapter written by the political scientist Bernard Brodie, which have come to be considered a founding document of American nuclear strategy, and which we may take as representative of the second school of thought. Brodie begins by accepting as given the continuation of the sovereign state—the very thing whose abolition Einstein saw as the only hope for survival in the nuclear world. As befits someone stating a premise, Brodie does not so much argue the point as simply assert it, saying, with light irony, that "the wholesale conversion of mankind away from those parochial attitudes bound up in nationalism is a consummation devoutly to be wished" but "the mere existence of the bomb does not promise to accomplish it at an early enough time to be of any use." If the existence of the nation-state is a given, then the possibility of the use of force becomes another given, because it is through the use of force that nations have ultimately sought to assure their survival. And if the possibility of the use of force is a given, then the existence of nuclear weapons becomes still another given, because nuclear weapons are the most powerful instruments of force available. Thus, while it may be true that, as Einstein said, if you want to rid the world of nuclear weapons you will have to establish a world government, neither of these things, in Brodie's view, can be accomplished, and the truly important and interesting question, therefore, is what policy to adopt in a world in which both sovereign states and nuclear weapons are present. Significantly, Brodie does not see this task as an end in itself; rather, he sees it as a way of buying time while more radical solutions, of the Einsteinian variety, are worked on. He wants merely to "transmute what appears to be an immediate crisis into a long-term problem," so as to give society the opportunity it needs to adjust its politics to its physics. His answer to the problem of mismatched timing is to work within the realm of the politically "possible" for the present, and postpone more ambitious efforts. It is noteworthy, though, that while he and the other authors of *The Absolute Weapon* acknowledge the need to find radical solutions sometime in the future they have no suggestions to offer about how to proceed with this work. The "short term" occupies them completely.

It is in framing policy for a world in which nuclear weapons are a given that Brodie shows his prescience and his originality. He begins with an unsparing description of the destructive power of the atomic bomb—a description that Einstein, for one, would surely have approved of. He points out that to destroy any city in the world, from one to ten atomic, or fission, bombs will suffice (the hydrogen, or fusion, bomb, which can be thousands of times as powerful as the fission bomb, and so can do the job much more efficiently, had, of course, not yet been invented); that no defense against the bomb is possible; and therefore "it is now physically possible for air forces no greater than those existing in the recent war to wipe out all the cities of a great nation in a single day." He then notes that some "scientists and laymen" who have a "passionate" preoccupation with "proposals for 'world government' " have concluded from these admittedly terrifying facts that "the safeguards to security formerly provided by military might are no longer of any use," and that the bomb must therefore be regarded as "the apotheosis of aggressive instruments." And he quotes J. Robert Oppenheimer as saying that the bomb "is a weapon for aggressors, and the elements of surprise and of terror are as intrinsic to it as are the fissionable nuclei." Brodie disagrees. In a key paragraph, he says, "The truth of Professor Oppenheimer's statement depends on one vital but unexpressed assumption: that the nation which proposes to launch the attack will not need to fear retaliation. If it must fear retaliation, the fact that it destroys its opponent's cities some hours or even days before its own are destroyed may avail it little.'' The would-be aggressor, who knew that he faced retaliation, Brodie thinks, would very likely give up its aggression. ''Multilateral possession of the bomb,'' therefore, will discourage, not encourage, aggression, provided that it is ''as nearly certain as possible that the aggressor who uses the bomb will have it used against him.''

Here, in a nutshell, and without the jargon and intellectual adornment of the ''strategic theory'' that unfolded luxuriantly in later years, is the doctrine of nuclear deterrence—although Brodie did not use that word. From Brodie's observations flowed the basic tenets of the doctrine of deterrence: that nuclear weapons offer nations effectively unlimited force; that winning a nuclear war is impossible; that it is imperative, therefore, to stop such a war from ever beginning; that the weapons themselves play the crucial role in that effort; that an invulnerable retaliatory force is of particular importance; that there is a special danger inherent in any capacity, on either side, for destroying the nuclear forces of the other side in a first strike; and that ''perceptions'' and ''psychology'' play an essential role in convincing the adversary that any aggression by him will lead only to his annihilation, and so in maintaining the ''stability'' of the whole arrangement. Summing up in a way that must have been jarring to military sensibilities at that time, Brodie wrote, ''The writer . . . is not for the moment concerned about who will *win* the next war in which atomic bombs are used. Thus far the chief purpose of our military establishment has been to win wars. From now on its chief purpose must be to avert them. It can have almost no other useful purpose.'' The policy of deterrence did not, of course, remove the peril of nuclear annihilation. On the contrary, it deliberately and firmly increased it (by sanctioning a buildup of nuclear arms), in the hope that the immediacy of the threat, felt by each side in the face of the other side's nuclear arsenals, would produce a stalemate in which the world would live on the very edge of the abyss but for precisely that reason would take special care not to lose its balance. The great advantage of deterrence was not the high degree of safety that it offered—for under it a single miscalculation could tip the world into the abyss—but its immediate practicability. For while it was doubtful in the extreme that the world would soon put together a world government, there was little doubt that in the absence of such a step the world's great powers could and would build large nuclear arsenals and threaten one another with them. To be sure, once the Soviet Union had acquired nuclear weapons, and the nuclear stalemate had been established, no one in either Washington or Moscow needed any political scientists to tell him that a nuclear attack might be met with retaliation in kind, and was, for that reason, among other, a bad idea. But it was the distinction of Brodie and his fellow-strategists to foresee this in 1946, when only one power possessed the bomb. His discovery was that a balance of nuclear forces might make possible a world more stable than any before it in our century. While he agreed with the advocates of world government that the bomb could not be defended against, he saw, as many of them did not, that the threat of retaliation could play the role that defenses had played in the past, and that in

46

this threat there might lie a measure of safety for a nuclear-armed world.

The argument between the Einsteinian school and the Brodiean school reflected not just a split in opinion but a split in the world itself. For the arrival of nuclear weapons in the world had at a stroke opened a fissure down the center of human life, placing whole realms of human existence at odds with one another. The traditional demands of man's international political existence, rooted in sovereignty and pursued through the use of force, were suddenly at variance with the demands of man's existence pure and simple, which was now mortally endangered. Political man held a knife to the throat of biological man, but since politics, like every other human activity, is possible only where there are human beings, political man also held a knife to his own throat. At the same time, the demands of man's moral existence, which were meaningless if they did not call on us to hold back at all costs from slaughtering billions of people and perhaps putting our species to death, were at variance with those of man's political existence, which seemed to require that we threaten to do just that, on pain of military defeat by our enemies if we did not. Einstein and Brodie, in a manner of speaking, took up positions on opposite sides of the gap, with Einstein standing alongside trembling, imperilled biological man and asking political man to yield, and Brodie standing alongside dug-in, unbudgeable political man and asking biological man to endure the peril. And each, of course, had a compelling reason for standing where he did, since no one could deny, on the one hand, that the peril was great—indeed, unlimited—and its urgency extreme or, on the other, that the immediate top-to-bottom transformation of international political life was, at the very least, doubtful. A bystander looking for guidance was left to contemplate two conclusions, each of which had apparently been established incontrovertibly by experts: (1) that the nature of physical reality as it had now been revealed by physics made a swift revolution in global politics necessary if human survival was to be assured, and (2) that the nature of political reality as it had revealed itself throughout history made such a revolution impossible.

People of Einstein's persuasion came to be called "idealists," as he had noted, while those of Brodie's persuasion came to be called "realists," but in fact both camps were characterized by a spirit of realism. This was not a debate in which there was reality on one side and a mistaken idea on the other. Rather, there were two opposed realities: the reality of the peril of extinction by nuclear arms, and the reality of the existing political institutions of the world. The two schools of thought therefore did not so much clash irreconcilably as fail even to join the argument; it was as though each were addressing a different "nuclear predicament"—and, in a way, each was. Einstein took as his point of departure his knowledge of the laws of physics and of the peril they defined; he went on to ask what had to be done to remove the peril, and concluded that the whole political realm had to be revolutionized. Since not only politics but everything human was in danger of "being disintegrated someday into atoms and swept up into the atmosphere," as he put it, revolution in just one department of life seemed to him a small price to pay. Brodie, by contrast, took as his point of departure his knowledge of the laws of politics and of the existing political world, and concluded that for the immediate future the peril would have to be lived with. Rarely in a great debate had each side had so many seemingly incontestable points to make. Could anyone seriously doubt that, as a supporter of Einstein's views said, quoting Alexander Hamilton, "to look for a continuation of harmony between a number of independent, unconnected sovereignties situated in the same neighborhood would be to disregard the uniform course of human events, and to set at defiance the accumulated experience of ages"? On the other hand, could anyone argue with William T. R. Fox, one of the authors of *The Absolute Weapon*, when, in the final chapter of that book, he observed, "It would be very dangerous to create a machine of central force before one created a machinery of central justice. For a machinery of central justice to work satisfactorily, its judgments would have to be based upon a worldwide community of values. That community of values does not exist today"? Wasn't it a fact that, as Einstein said, "today the atomic bomb has altered profoundly the nature of the world as we know it, and the human race consequently finds itself in a new habitat to which it must adapt its thinking"? But wasn't it also a fact that, as Fox noted, a Soviet commentator had just called the idea of world government a smoke screen for "renunciation of the basis of the struggle against fascist aggression"; and that the United States was also "unwilling to surrender a degree of control over its own destinies sufficient to permit a world authority to enforce its declared policy against any challenger"?

Einstein and Brodie, each rooted firmly in the reality

he knew best, were unable to find common ground. Einstein, the proponent of what was necessary for survival, could not persuade the world that it was politically possible. Brodie the definer of what was politically possible, could not enlarge his conception of it to encompass what was necessary for survival. The world was offered two problematic proposals: one that would solve the problem but could not be brought into being, and one that could be brought into being but did not solve the problem. The gap between them—between imperilled biological man and entrenched political man; between the irresistible force of nuclear weapons and the immovable object of the world's political institutions (immovable, that is, except by nuclear weapons, which could move them right out of existence in an instant); between a resolution of the broad human crisis of the peril of extinction and a resolution of the political crisis of how the world was to be organized without war; between the laws of science and the laws of history; between the dictates of conscience and the dictates of policy; between "idealism" and "realism"; between the "long term" and the "short term"; between the necessary and the possible; between the slowness of political change and the swiftness of the approach of doom—remained unbridged. And it has remained so to the present day.

Whoever may have had the better of the debate between the two schools, it was, of course, the deterrence doctrine that eventually became official policy. People couldn't, or wouldn't, or just did not, establish world government, and they turned to the only prominent alternative. Before that happened, however, the United

States launched an initiative at the United Nations to prevent a nuclear-arms race and abolish nuclear weapons. The initiative failed, but in failing it threw a spotlight on the mountainous political obstacles to a solution of the nuclear problem. The initiative originated, in January of 1946, with the appointment by Secretary of State James Byrnes of a committee headed by Under-Secretary of State Dean Acheson whose work would be to frame a proposal for nuclear disarmament which the United States would make at a forthcoming meeting of the Atomic Energy Commission of the United Nations. Acheson proceeded to appoint a board of consultants, under the chairmanship of David E. Lilienthal, who was then the director of the Tennessee Valley Authority, and including Robert Oppenheimer. On March 17, after intense labors, the committee and the board of consultants concluded their deliberations and embodied them in a document commonly known as the Acheson-Lilienthal report, which was transmitted to Byrnes the following day. At the heart of the committee's recommendations was a proposal that nuclear activities be placed under international control. The report had arrived at an ingenious solution (which may yet prove useful to the world one day) to the thorny problem arising from the need for inspection under any agreement by nations to forgo the production and possession of nuclear arms. Impressed by the political difficulties that would face teams charged with inspecting a large number of independent, national nuclear facilities, the report recommended that all "dangerous" nuclear activities—from uranium mining to the construction of nuclear reactors—be placed under the direct ownership of an international authority associated with the United

Nations. (Individual nations would be licensed by the authority to carry out certain "safe" nuclear activities.) This authority, they reasoned, could readily inspect that which it was doing itself.

On March 18, President Truman announced the appointment of Bernard Baruch, a financier who served as an adviser to several Presidents, to represent the United States at the disarmament talks at the United Nations, and Baruch was given the Acheson–Lilienthal report. Much to the dismay of the report's authors, Baruch turned out to have many reservations about it, including its assumption that major violations of the proposed system of international controls would ultimately come before the United Nations Security Council, whose decisions could be nullified by a veto by any one of five nations: the United States, the Soviet Union, England, France, and China. It was the Soviet veto that worried Baruch. He recommended that the veto power in the Security Council be abolished for decisions having to do with atomic energy. And, in a second major departure from the report, he recommended that penalties be established for violations of the agreement concerning atomic energy. (The report had not proposed any penalties.) Without these, he said, the proposal as a whole would amount to nothing more than a warning system, which would put the world on notice if nuclear arming began but would be unable to do anything about it. In short, he had noted the lack in the report of any means for dealing with the underlying political question of how disputes among nations—in this case, disputes concerning the life-and-death matter of atomic energy— were to be decided, and his recommendations were designed to repair the omission: the Security Council would decide. What he recommended was not world government, but it contained something like the essence of world government: an authority with the power to make and enforce decisions concerning the most critical element of military power. President Truman agreed with Baruch and adopted his recommendations.

In June, Baruch presented the proposal to the United Nations, and it was immediately turned down by Andrei Gromyko, the Soviet representative at the arms negotiations. The Soviet Union had substantial reasons for turning it down. The United Nations, which did not yet include most of the hundred-odd nations that make up what we now call the Third World, could be counted on in those days to vote in favor of Western proposals, and the Soviet Union's veto in the Security Council was its only means of undoing the results. To accept an international authority that controlled mining rights in the Soviet Union and held a monopoly on nuclear energy could thus mean accepting not only a large measure of American control over Soviet nuclear energy but also American intervention in Soviet life—an idea as repugnant to the Soviet Union as the converse would have been to the United States if the Soviet Union had enjoyed majority support at the United Nations. Besides, the Soviet Union was at the time well on its way to getting the bomb. (It succeeded in 1949.) However, the Soviet Union went far beyond rejecting the repeal of the veto. It also denounced inspection, as a breach of national sovereignty. Gromyko stated, ''When the Charter of the United Nations was prepared by the conference at San Francisco, the question of sovereignty was one of the most important questions considered. This principle of sovereignty is one of the cornerstones on which the United Nations structure is built; if this were touched the whole existence and future of the United Nations would be threatened.'' But Gromyko did not go on to suggest ways in which the Baruch plan could be made acceptable. Instead, he made a proposal that seemed almost designed to be unacceptable to the United States—as we may suspect that it was, given the Soviet Union's strong interest in developing the bomb for itself, and its imminent ability to do so. Gromyko called for an international convention to ban the production of nuclear weapons, which was to be followed some time later by the establishment of two committees at the United Nations—one for an exchange of scientific information, and the other to fashion safeguards for the abolition agreement. In short, the United States was *first* to give up its atomic monopoly, and *then* the Soviet Union would consent to *discuss* inspection and international control. The predictable United States rejection came quickly.

The amendment of the Acheson-Lilienthal report by Baruch, and then the rejection of the Baruch proposal by the Soviet Union—accompanied by a wholly unacceptable proposal of its own—illustrated the likely fate of any plan, however brilliant, that did not take into account the political questions at the outset. Once again—this time in action rather than in theory—the world had reached the impasse that seemed to block any radical or full solution of the nuclear predicament. The Acheson-Lilienthal committee had repaired to the relatively uncontroversial ground of technology, and offered a technical solution to the problem. But the problem could not in fact be divorced from the political issue, which meant at bottom how the world was going to be making its decisions in the international arena from then on, and the two governments, whose very business was politics, had no choice but to put politics back into the negotiations. When they did that, however, the proposal foundered, because there was no willingness on either side to make the radical political concessions that alone could have put the two sides on negotiable ground. It was as though in the course of the negotiations they had recognized the validity of Einstein's conviction that the predicament could be resolved only if a global authority with real power was established. But the plain truth, as William T. R. Fox had noted in *The Absolute Weapon*, was that neither side wanted a real international authority—not presiding over nuclear matters, and not presiding over any other matters, either—whose actions it could neither control nor derail. (When the United States lost its majority support at the United Nations, it quickly lost its enthusiasm for the idea that any binding decisions should be made by that body.) Both sides preferred a nuclear-arms race, with the United States hoping to use its technical superiority to increase its lead, and the Soviet Union hoping to catch up. (As was virtually inevitable, the latter is what eventually happened.)

The arms race began. Other proposals for full nuclear disarmament were made, but they never occupied the center of the political stage. Much of what Brodie and other advocates of deterrence had foreseen for a nuclear-armed world came to pass. In the succeeding decades, no war, conventional or nuclear—much less a third world war—broke out between the great nuclear powers. Whether war was avoided because of the balance of terror or for some other reason we cannot know (a negative is impossible to prove), but it is only common sense to suppose that the fear of nuclear destruction, while it was not the only factor involved, contributed heavily to the resolve of the great powers to remain at peace. However, another of Brodie's hopes went unfulfilled—his hope that deterrence would serve as a stopgap to buy time in which the world could find its way to the long-term political solution he saw as ultimately necessary. For many years, deterrence continued to be explained as a time-buying measure. As late as 1960, for example, Herman Kahn, a prominent theorist of nuclear strategy, was arguing for a policy of deterrence by saying, ''We must take seriously the problem of reaching 1975.'' The possibility of a long-term solution still seemed real to him, and in 1962 he wrote:

We probably must accept the notion that the world as we know it is passing from the stage of history, and that attempts to preserve this five-hundred-year-old nation-state system would probably be as futile as the earlier attempts of some of the small German or Italian states to stave off the unification of their countries. If we wish to influence these coming changes, we simply must learn much more about existing and potential international orders—and learn fast.

But none of the sweeping changes occurred, or even began to occur—not after 1946, not after 1960, and not after the world had made it to 1975. The short term had a way of stretching on indefinitely and the long term a way of receding into the future. Deterrence had been presented as a sort of trailer that mankind would live in while the permanent home of a full political resolution of the nuclear predicament was being constructed. But what happened as the years passed was that the trailer was built up and elaborated, while the home went unstarted.

The failure of the long term ever to arrive was no small defect in the justification for the doctrine of deterrence, inasmuch as it had been in considerable measure by presenting deterrence as a short-term, time-buying device that its advocates had answered objections to the doctrine's glaring shortcomings: that it held mankind perpetually dangling over the nuclear abyss, suspended on the slender thread of whatever wisdom the statesmen, all of them fallible, and many of them extremely so, might happen to possess at a given instant; that by defining safety in terms of possessing nuclear arsenals it not only permitted but actually encouraged their proliferation; that it kept us all in the intolerable position of standing ready to slaughter billions of our fellow human beings; and, in general, that it required us all to rely for our safety on the criminal and absurd "threat" to blow our species off the face of the earth forever. What the world actually experienced was not the hoped-for slow progress toward a full solution but steady retrogression, in the form of the arms race and the proliferation of nuclear weapons, which were developed by more and more countries. Sometimes our performance in the postwar period is called a great success, on the ground that we have so far avoided a nuclear holocaust, and much of the credit for the success is given to the policy of deterrence. What this reckoning overlooks is that in that same period the world has built up arsenals of more than fifty thousand nuclear warheads—in short, that behind the screen of our deterrence policy we have built the means of our annihilation. Seen in the best possible light, this self-endangerment of our species was a tragic necessity. Seen less forgivingly—and, I believe, more justly—it was the greatest collective failure of responsibility by any generation in history. But, whichever of these it was, self-congratulation is certainly out of order. If someone climbs out on the ledge of a high building and threatens to jump off, we do not stand around congratulating him on his wisdom and restraint in not having jumped yet, and expounding on how safe a place the ledge of a building must be; we seek to pull him in at the earliest possible opportunity.

Part of the nuclear buildup was sanctioned—in fact, required—by the doctrine of deterrence, which founded the world's safety not on Einstein's "law and order" but on terror. To that extent, deterrence must share in the blame for our suicidal preparations. But the nuclear buildup—apparently fuelled by a tremendous internal momentum—went far, far beyond what was required under that doctrine. Strictly speaking, the deterrence doctrine should have set a limit on the number of bombs required by a nation. It would have been the number needed to guarantee the destruction of the adversary's society in a retaliatory strike. Brodie wrote in 1946, "It appears that for any conflict a specific number of bombs will be useful to the side using it, and anything beyond that will be a luxury. . . . We can say that if two thousand bombs in the hands of either party is enough to destroy entirely the economy of the other, the fact that one side has six thousand and the other two thousand will be of relatively small significance.'' This is another idea of Brodie's that went unnoticed. Instead of stopping the arms race when several thousand Hiroshima-sized weapons had been stockpiled on each side, the super-powers invented the hydrogen bomb and went on to build tens of thousands of those, giving each side the preposterously redundant capacity for raining down hundreds of thousands of Hiroshimas on the adversary. Deterrence theory, it seemed, was competent to start an arms race but not to stop one.

There was a retrogression in thinking as well. While the nuclear arsenals grew to tower up to the sky around us, people seemed to forget that anyone had ever hoped for any other kind of world. People got accustomed to life in the trailer and forgot about the permanent home they were supposed to have had. Intellectual horizons narrowed and hopes dimmed. The version of a world without nuclear weapons all but died. People's eyes became adjusted to the nuclear darkness, in a sort of moral equivalent of the nuclear winter. The time that Brodie had hoped to win was won, but it had not been used to achieve the ends he had had in mind. Instead, the champions of deterrence lost their former modesty and began to advance their makeshift plans as a permanent solution. The journalist Thomas Powers has spoken in the past few years to many of the military men who are responsible for carrying out the nuclear policies of the United States, and he has made a special point of asking them how they view the future. In his recent book *Thinking About the Next War*, he reports that he found two convictions to be nearly universal: first, that even with the arsenals in place—in fact, *because* the arsenals are in place—nuclear weapons will *never* be used and, second, that the military men "*know* we shall never get rid of nuclear weapons": that their abolition not only is "not on the horizon" but is not even "*over* the horizon." That is also the view of the Harvard authors of *Living with Nuclear Weapons,* who ask, "Why not abolish nuclear weapons? Why not cleanse this small planet of these deadly poisons?" They answer categorically, "Because we cannot," and go on to explain that the discovery of nuclear weapons "lies behind us" and "cannot be undone." In this prognosis, the hope of abolishing nuclear weapons has been extinguished, and the short-term stopgap of deterrence has completely usurped the place of full nuclear disarmament, which is frankly ruled out.

The doctrine of deterrence reigned supreme in official circles in the United States for the better part of the postwar period, during which the public, for its part, showed only sporadic interest in nuclear matters—being only too willing, it seemed, to hand the whole sickening business over to the specialists. Then, toward the end of the 1970s, this wide consensus—consisting, on the one hand, of widespread doctrinal agreement among government officials and, on the other, of public acceptance of their stewardship—was unexpectedly shattered by two upheavals: one in public opinion, in the form of the new peace movement, and the other in government policy, in the form of a subtle but profound and many-sided crisis in the doctrine of deterrence itself, which is now in a state of confusion amounting almost to disintegration. And this confusion, in turn, forced the world to face once again the elemental questions that

Brodie and Einstein, among many others, had confronted, but not resolved, in the first days of the nuclear age. Even as the doctrine's theorists were elevating it to the position of dogmatic truth, support for it was beginning to erode. As so often seems to happen in the history of both men and ideas, the moment of apotheosis was the signal for decline. The crisis in the doctrine emerged into full public view under the Reagan Administration, but cracks had been appearing in it for at least half a decade before that. As the balance prescribed by deterrence was attained (with lots of overkill thrown in for good measure), contradictions that had always underlain the doctrine but had gone largely unremarked on before began to emerge into prominence. These contradictions all had to do, in one way or another, with the central, unresolvable contradiction of "defending" one's country by threatening to use weapons whose actual use would bring on the annihilation of one's country and possibly of the world as well. And the emergence of the contradictions was in turn propelled, I believe, by a recognition—this time on the part of nuclear strategists rather than citizens at large—of what a doomsday machine really is, and what it means to intend, in certain circumstances, to use one. This gigantic new reality, which has quietly grown up behind our backs in the decades since the weapons were invented, is, I suggest, the underlying cause of both the crisis in public confidence and the crisis in policy, and so in that sense they are part of a single, deeper crisis. Both, in their different ways, are responses to the fantastic, horrifying, brutal, and absurd fact that we human beings have actually gone ahead and wired our planet for its and our destruction. Whereas for the public, which was not much interested in the subtleties of doctrine, the crisis appeared in the stark form of the over-all senselessness and horror of the species' highly advanced preparations to commit suicide, for the strategists it took the form of a thousand inconsistencies, anomalies, and logical faults that kept cropping up irrepressibly in the details of nuclear policies and in their justifications. Yet when these various internal faults are looked at closely they turn out to be symptoms of the larger absurdity that is upsetting the public.

According to strict deterrence theory, the attainment of parity over the years should have had a stabilizing effect, for only then did the deterrence system become fully operational. The world should have breathed easier. Superiority on either side, theory decreed, lessens the security of both, because it creates an incentive on the stronger side to strike first, which, in turn, creates an incentive on the weaker side to avoid that first strike by itself striking first, and so on. When the strategists actually found themselves looking at parity, however, they discovered that it made them nervous. For one thing, parity put in question several American policies of long standing, perhaps the most important being the policy for the defense of Europe, where, in the opinion of many experts, the Soviet Union enjoyed superiority in conventional forces. In the event of a Soviet conventional attack in Europe, the American plan was—and still is—to make up for NATO's possible conventional inferiority by resorting to nuclear weapons early in the hostilities. (The American reliance on nuclear weapons to defend Europe goes back to the first years of the postwar period, when the United States had a monopoly on nuclear weapons and, in response to strong public demand, had partly demobilized the conventional forces that had been fighting in the Second World War.) As long as the United States possessed clear nuclear superiority, it could be argued that this plan had a certain plausibility—or "credibility," to use the favored term—because it was at least possible to imagine that if the Soviet Union was faced with a nuclear attack in Europe it would refrain from responding in kind, for fear of coming off worse in a general holocaust. But when the Soviet Union reached nuclear parity with the United States this thinking no longer obtained. Then there remained no basis (in deterrence theory, at any rate) for believing that the Soviet Union would hold back from nuclear retaliation if the United States had used nuclear weapons first. And if after that Soviet retaliation the United States attacked again, at a higher level of force, there was no reason to suppose that the Soviet Union would not retaliate in kind again, and so on up the line, until both sides' arsenals were depleted and both sides were annihilated. While one supposed virtue of nuclear superiority was that with it you could get an advantage in a war, it also had another theoretical virtue, which was that it might supply a stopping point in any hostilities that got going—the point at which the weaker side, foreseeing the unfavorable consequences to itself of continuing, gave up. But when the forces became equal that point would never be arrived at and the escalation would climb smoothly to oblivion. In the succinct (if ungrammatical) words of Henry Kissinger in an address in Brussels in 1979, which were quoted recently by former Secretary of Defense Robert McNamara in an article on NATO's nuclear policy, and on the role of nuclear weapons in general, in *Foreign Affairs*, "the

European allies should not keep asking us to multiply strategic assurances that we cannot possibly mean, or if we do mean, we should not want to execute because if we execute, we risk the destruction of civilization." And, in Mr. McNamara's own words in the article, "if deterrence fails and conflict develops, the present NATO strategy carries with it a high risk that Western civilization, as we know it, will be destroyed"—to which one can add that *Homo sapiens* in its entirety may be destroyed into the bargain.

At the outset of a crisis, it is true, the President may not have to make the final, drastic choice. The policy of "flexible response"—of responding to each level of attack with a comparable level of retaliation—offers him less drastic steps to take. And certainly we should hope that even after the madness has begun it can somehow be stopped. (One excellent proposal that has been made recently is for a joint Soviet-American control center, where in the event of a crisis information could be exchanged, so that the two powers wouldn't miscalculate one another's intentions.) However, flexible response, even if it works, can only postpone, not evade, that final decision. If the foe is determined—and we have to assume that he is if he has launched a nuclear war against a nuclear-armed adversary—then the moment will still come, after the "limited" salvos have been fired, when a choice must be made between defeat and annihilation. But that moment may come well before some of the scenarists of nuclear war imagine that it will come, for there is good reason to doubt where the limited attacks supposedly made available by flexible response will stay limited. The hope that nuclear hostilities, once they are started, can be limited depends on at least four very doubtful assumptions: that the leaders on both sides will retain control over their forces and that their orders will be obeyed (if, that is, the leaders survive); that the adversary will grasp one's "limited" intent even as he sees nuclear bombs tearing up his armies and his country; that if he does grasp this he will, in the interests of restraint all around, forgo the real or imagined advantages of a full-scale preemptive strike; and, finally, that the two sides, showing a wisdom in the midst of a nuclear holocaust which they failed to show in the days and hours leading up to it, while the world was intact, will come to their senses, establish diplomatic contact, and agree to halt the descent into the abyss in mid-course. No one knows how diplomacy would fare halfway to the end of the world, but it seems unwise to rely on it very heavily. In any case, the conclusion that the nuclear winter may descend after only a fraction of the world's present arsenals have been detonated may have made the distinction between "limited" and "total" nuclear war academic. "Limited war" itself has turned out to have potentially unlimited consequences.

In an effort to remedy the flaws in the American plan for the defense of Europe, the NATO governments hit on a plan that turned out only to exacerbate the underlying tensions. If the American threat to defend Europe with nuclear weapons was losing credibility, the NATO planners feared, then the Soviet leaders might start to believe that they could conquer or intimidate Europe without encountering an American response. This fear was increased when the Soviet Union began to withdraw its one-warhead SS-4 intermediate-range missiles that it had targeted on Europe and replace them with more modern, three-warhead SS-20 missiles. What was needed, the NATO planners decided—both to "reassure" the Europeans and to frighten the Russians—was a way of binding the defense of Europe more tightly to the defense of the United States. The upshot was the Euromissiles—intermediate-range ballistic and cruise missiles that would be based in Europe and would be capable of striking the Soviet Union. Their deployment, it was believed, would convince the Soviet Union once and for all that the Americans were serious about the defense of Europe. The problem was that a mere change in the place of deployment—from the United States to Europe—of American missiles capable of reaching Soviet territory did little to cure the incredibility of the threat of their use. In Mr. McNamara's words, "for the same reason that led Henry Kissinger to recognize that a U.S. President is unlikely to initiate the use of U.S.-based strategic nuclear weapons against the U.S.S.R., so a President would be unlikely to launch missiles from European soil against Soviet territory." Meanwhile, a large segment of the European citizenry was anything but reassured by the plan. On the contrary, it was frightened. People in Europe felt that they were becoming all too dependent on the United States, and they feared that the United States might drag them against their will into a holocaust of its own making. They believed that they were becoming (in the recent words of Rudolf Augstein, the publisher of *Der Spiegel*) a "computer component" in a broader superpower game, over which they had no control. Furthermore, unconvinced that the Euromissiles, which were to be under the sole control of the United States, would bind the fortunes of Europe and the United States closer together, they feared that the missiles might be used to try to fight a "limited" nuclear war in Europe alone, sparing the United States. (These fears were fanned when President Reagan opined at a briefing for news editors in October of 1981 that a limited nuclear war might indeed be possible.) Before long, a very large number of these people began to make their apprehensions known in demonstrations throughout Europe.

Meanwhile, in the United States four Americans with long experience in government—George Kennan; McGeorge Bundy; Gerard Smith, head of the delegation that negotiated the SALT I agreement; and Robert McNamara—had a quite different solution to suggest to the problem of the defense of Europe. They recommended that the United States consider adopting a policy of no first use of nuclear weapons in Europe while building NATO conventional forces to whatever level was necessary to achieve a balance with Warsaw Pact conventional forces. As they saw it, a policy of no first use would improve on the existing policy in a number of ways; it would add to the credibility of an American response to Soviet conventional attack (since at least the initial American response would no longer have to be suicidal); it would remove from the United States the responsibility and the onus of actually planning to be the first to use nuclear weapons (the Soviets have already declared a no-first-use policy); it would, by giving the United States something better to do in the event of aggression in Europe than start a nuclear holocaust, somewhat reduce the chances of a holocaust. These benefits, all of which appear to be real and substantial, are perhaps reason enough to adopt the policy of no first use, yet that policy would nevertheless fall short of fully resolving the contradiction that underlies the American plan for the defense of Europe. In conventional war, there is no guarantee of success in any engagement—and certainly not when the opposing forces are, by design, evenly balanced. Hence, in the event that a conventional war broke out in Europe it is quite possible that, even if there should be a conventional balance in place, the NATO forces would begin to lose, and so would be forced to decide anyway between defeat and a first use of nuclear weapons—or, if the Warsaw Pact started to lose, it would face the decision. In either case, there seems to be a fair chance that nuclear weapons would be used. Conventional defeat is the Achilles' heel of no first use. A policy of no first use thus can never really live up to its name. There is always an invisible asterisk attached, referring us to a footnote that reads, "Unless we start to lose." Without this qualification, a policy of no first use would really be a form of unilateral nuclear disarmament by verbal means, in which the foe was invited to take what he could, provided only that he did it with conventional forces. (If he used nuclear forces, nuclear deterrence would come into play.)

This limitation of no first use, of which the authors of the proposal were well aware, is worth mentioning not because it discredits the recommendation (it does not) but because it points to the contradiction at the heart of deterrence itself. The underlying problem, which both citizens and policymakers are now wrestling with, is that, given the difficulty of limiting nuclear war, and given the extreme consequences even if the war *is* limited, *any* actual use of nuclear weapons is likely to be self-defeating and senseless. For whether or not there is a policy of no first use, and whether or not the hostilities begin with the use of conventional weapons, there is, ultimately, no way to spare the President (if it is he who faces the decision) from having to make the final, terrible choice between defeat and annihilation. This is the moment at which the President has to decide whether or not actually to carry out the notorious "threat of suicide"—also known as the "threat to end the world"—with which the two great nuclear powers ultimately hope to deter one another from aggression. (Deployment of the Euromissiles commits him to making it earlier rather than later.) The crux of the matter is that while there may be a benefit in making the threat it can never make sense to carry it out, no matter what the circumstances. For how can it make sense to "save" one's country by blowing it to pieces? And what logic is there in staving off a limited defeat by bringing on unlimited, eternal defeat? Nuclear deterrence is like a gun with two barrels, of which one points ahead and the other points back at the gun's holder. If a burglar should enter your house, it might make sense to threaten him with this gun, but it could never make sense to fire it.

The dilemma is even more sharply defined if one turns from Europe, where the West has conventional forces in place with which to at least try to repel possible Soviet aggression, to the Middle East, where it has almost none and, furthermore, has no chance of dispatching enough in time to make a military difference. The fault line in the doctrine here is wider. In the Middle East, the military policy is either one of nuclear first use or nothing. The United States is making provision for a rapid-deployment force that could be sent to the Middle East in a crisis, but in the face of a full-scale

Soviet conventional attack it could do no more than be a trip wire for the American launching of nuclear weapons. Yet the Soviet Union can retaliate with nuclear weapons in the Middle East just as easily as it can in Europe, and the ladder of escalation climbs up just as smoothly from the Persian Gulf as it does from the plains of Germany. The President appears to have no way to "protect" Middle Eastern oil militarily other than by launching nuclear weapons. But for whose use will the oil have been protected if everyone winds up dead in the process of protecting it?

If the threat of nuclear war is irrational, one might ask, why do nations go on making it, and why do they bother even to build nuclear weapons instead of, say, building more conventional weapons, which, according to some theorists, they might sensibly use? Why doesn't the absurdity of "defending" one's country by threatening suicide lead to the collapse or abandonment of the policy? The answer, of course, is that the minute a nation gives up nuclear weapons it puts itself militarily at the mercy of its nuclear-armed foes, for no one has yet devised a successful defense against nuclear attack. Rather than be put in this position, nations prefer to make irrational threats—and hope never to be forced to decide whether or not to carry them out. As for the problem of credibility, in the real world—as opposed to the world of logic and theory—the irrationality of the threat to commit suicide probably doesn't do a great deal to reduce its effectiveness. There has been enough insanity in history to lend credibility to even the maddest threats, and for governments to threaten to do something irrational is quite enough to get everybody to believe they will do it. (It is one of the humiliating aspects of our nuclear policy that if rationality ever prevailed in the world our policy would become untenable.) Another point in favor of the deterrence doctrine is its probable descriptive honesty. It discards all dubious assumptions regarding the likelihood of limiting a nuclear holocaust; or, at the very least, it acknowledges that no sensible statesman can *count on* these assumptions, and therefore invites statesmen to look on the use of nuclear weapons as the beginning of the end. The morality of the doctrine of mutual assured destruction has been assailed on the ground that it calls for the mass slaughter of innocents, as indeed it does. But this immorality is inherent in the very possession of tens of thousands of nuclear weapons, whatever the doctrine. There is no conceivable way that these can be used without mass slaughter on an incalculable scale, and no theoretical sophistry can eliminate this basic fact. The doctrine of mutual assured destruction is in that sense not so much a policy as an acknowledgment of reality. It brings us— statesman and citizen alike—face to face with the way things really are in a nuclear-armed world.

In an article in *The New York Review of Books*, in June of 1983, McGeorge Bundy proposed a policy of what he called "existential deterrence," in which we would make political use of some of the inherent qualities of nuclear arsenals. One of these qualities is uncertainty. He observes that "existing systems on both sides are now so powerful and varied that no political leader can have or hope to have any clear idea of what would in fact happen 'if deterrence failed'—that is, if nuclear war began." And he goes on to remark that "scenarios" that pretend to predict what would happen "reflect nothing more than the state of mind of their authors." Our knowledge of the immense destructive power of nuclear weapons and our incurable ignorance of the exact course that that destruction would take are, he suggests, irreducible, "existential" properties of our nuclear arsenals, and he suggests that we can count on these properties to deter a foe, even without spelling out our murderous retaliatory intentions in detail. The reason for this uncertainty is, of course, the same as the reason for our uncertainty concerning our survival as a species "if deterrence failed": we have never had any experience with nuclear holocausts. The new findings that limited war could cause nuclear winter adds extremely important support to "existential" deterrence. This finding shows that an attacker might even destroy himself with his own first strike. Now, therefore our own missiles are not only figuratively but literally pointed at ourselves. But there is, of course, no cause for rejoicing in this, because while it is true that the new finding may make statesmen more reluctant than before to launch nuclear hostilities this gain is won at the cost of an increase in the danger of an accidental or inadvertent extinction of mankind.

Because of the "existential" properties of large nuclear arsenals, deterrence overcomes its cracked logical foundations and "works"; that is, it inspires a well-justified terror in the minds of our adversaries, just as their arsenals inspire a reciprocal terror in us. The illogic of deterrence does not lead to a direct weakening of the fear that it inspires. No statesman in his right mind is so foolish as to stake his country's existence on the surmise that if he launches a nuclear attack against his foe the foe, guided by pure reasonableness and logic, will sit back and endure the attack without responding. The consequences of the doctrine's illogic are to be found somewhere else: in another audience, in ourselves. This audience very much includes the people who make up the new peace movement—people who are increasingly repelled by the idea of putting mankind to the sword because some crisis in Europe or Lebanon or the Falkland Islands, or wherever, has got out of hand. But before the peace movement arose another group, close to power and more influential, had begun to ponder the dilemma. Its members were, and are, the strategists of "counterforce" and "nuclear-war-fighting," some of whom now guide the policies of the Reagan Administration. Having in many cases spent their lives studying nuclear strategy, they were well aware of the contradiction between the benefits of threatening to start a nuclear war and the senselessness of actually doing so. These people took theory seriously, and they took the contradiction seriously. They were not reassured by the uncertainty in nuclear affairs which restored the credibility that logic undermined, or by any of the other "existential" properties of nuclear arsenals. But what worried them chiefly was not, as with the peace movement, that a small crisis could bring on the end of the world; it was that the Soviet Union—counting on the reluctance of the United States to commit suicide by launching a nuclear attack—might go ahead with some act of aggression, including even a limited nuclear attack, hoping that there would be no response. But, having identified in deterrence the same inconsistency that the peace movement had identified, they struck off in an entirely different direction, embarking on a critique of mutual assured destruction from a new angle. The

73

new strategists wanted to repair American credibility, and in order to do it they set out to find some rational goal for the United States to pursue "if deterrence failed." How would the adversary be deterred, they asked, if there was no sensible or reasonable threat to deter him with? Their solution—which marked a radical shift in strategic thought—was the idea of actually fighting and winning a nuclear war, just as though it were a conventional war. If the United States could fight and win a nuclear war, then the *threat* to use nuclear weapons would no longer be a suicide threat, and would become credible again. Once the new thinking had found wide acceptance in the Reagan Administration, the Administration, without rejecting the doctrine of deterrence outright, began to make statements and take actions that could be interpreted only as part of a war-fighting, or war-winning, strategy. Navy Secretary John Lehman said, "You have to have a war-winning capability if you are to succeed." Secretary of Defense Caspar Weinberger said, "You show me a Secretary of Defense who's planning not to prevail [in a war], and I'll show you a Secretary of Defense who ought to be impeached." And, as I have mentioned, a top-secret plan stated that the United States should prepare to fight "a prolonged" nuclear war and to be able to "prevail" in it and "force the Soviet Union to seek earliest termination of hostilities on terms favorable to the United States."

A decision to "prevail" in the event of nuclear war necessarily wreaked havoc on the traditional tenets of deterrence. Deterrence called for equality of forces, but prevailing required superiority; deterrence was upset by the power of either side to destroy the forces of the other side in a first strike, but prevailing required such a power; deterrence acknowledged the impossibility of an effective defense against a nuclear attack, but prevailing required such a defense; deterrence sought stability and was consistent with arms-control agreements based on equality, but prevailing, since it required superiority, was inconsistent with such agreements. And the Reagan Administration set out to achieve the objectives required for prevailing. The President called for the development and deployment of first-strike weapons. His Administration proposed ambitious programs both for civil defense and for spacebased defense against Soviet ballistic missiles. All the while, it kept up a barrage of rhetoric against the Soviet Union more bellicose than anything heard from any other Administration in the postwar period.

As it happened, technical developments had for some time abetted the development by the United States of first-strike, nuclear-war-fighting weapons. One of these developments was the invention, in the mid-1960s, of the Multiple Independently Targeted Reentry Vehicle (MIRV), which permitted one missile to be equipped with many warheads, each of them guided to a different target. If the targets were the silos of enemy missiles, then just one missile fired offensively could menace many missiles sitting defensively in their silos. Another destabilizing technical development was a revolution in accuracy, which improved the chances that the warheads, multiplied or not, would actually reach the silos they aimed at. The doctrine of deterrence had always rested on the twin foundations of the vulnerability of civilian populations to nuclear attack and the invulnerability of nuclear forces to nuclear attack. But now offensive capacity was improving to a point at which nuclear forces were beginning to become vulnerable. Although bombers in the air and submarines at sea still remained safe from a first strike, the safety of land-based missiles was dwindling. Meanwhile, the Soviet Union, too, although its public statements were more restrained than those of the United States had become, was developing weapons with a first-strike capacity. The United States had been the first to deploy MIRVs but the Soviet Union was the first to place them on giant land-based missiles capable of carrying ten warheads apiece. (The MX, which will carry as many as ten warheads, is an attempt to match this dangerous achievement.) The move on both sides to build first-strike weapons shows the vulnerability of the nuclear balance in general to technical advances. The arms race is always, in effect, afloat on a stream of technical discovery, which can upset its most carefully laid plans. It is always as much a race against the scientific unknown as against the adversary per se. This aspect of the race— the qualitative, rather than the quantitative—has nothing to do with any malign influence of scientists. Rather, it is inherent in an arms race in a world in which experience has shown that the greatest advantages are to be gained not so much by mounting gigantic industrial efforts as by fishing new devices out of the unknown. At bottom, it stems from each side's well-justified fear that the other side will arrive at an advantageous discovery first. (An example would be a device that could detect the positions of submarines from a great distance.)

* * *

The debate between the mutual-assured-destruction school and the new nuclear-war-fighting school happens to have been encapsulated in an exchange of letters between the writer Theodore Draper and Secretary of Defense Weinberger in *The New York Review of Books*. (In entering into correspondence with Draper, Weinberger, as Draper acknowledged, showed a respect for the views of a private citizen—and, by implication, a sense of accountability to the public—that is all too often lacking in public officials.) It gives us a portrait in miniature of the stresses that are now tearing deterrence apart. The occasion for the exchange was an open letter written by Weinberger which appeared in *The New York Review* in November of 1982. In an "open reply," Draper takes note of the top-secret document, parts of which were obtained by the *New York Times*—"Fiscal Year 1984-1988 Defense Guidance," which was approved by Weinberger and provides general strategic direction over a five-year period for America's armed services—which states that American nuclear forces "must prevail and be able to force the Soviet Union to seek earliest termination of hostilities on terms favorable to the United States," and he goes on to accuse the Administration of planning to try to "win" a nuclear war. In a letter to Draper, Weinberger denies the charge, saying, "we believe neither side could win," and he also denies that the Administration hopes to "prevail" in a protracted nuclear war. But, going on to broach the question that has occasioned the rise of the nuclear-war-fighting school—namely, what the United States should actually do with its nuclear weapons "if deterrence fails"—he says, "U.S. contingency planning, to serve deterrence, must also envision the possible employment of nuclear weapons.'' The answer of the mutual-assured-destruction school to the question of what to do if deterrence fails is that one goes ahead with mutual assured destruction. This answer Weinberger rejects, explaining that ''it would be militarily, politically and morally unsound to confine the President to resorting either to capitulation or massive retaliation.'' Then, giving his own formulation of what to do he says, ''Our policy requires that, if necessary, we prevail in denying victory to the Soviets and in protecting the sovereignty and continued viability of the United States and of the Western democracies as free societies.'' But this goal—with its ''viability of the United States,'' its preserved ''sovereignty,'' its intact ''free societies,'' and its ''denying victory'' to the Soviet Union—has about it a suspicious look of prevailing, not to say winning.

Weinberger's tortured and evasive formulation gives Draper his opening to respond. In a second letter, he accuses Weinberger of rejecting the goal of prevailing at the beginning of his letter ''only to reinstate it in a peculiarly negative form''—in which the phrase ''terms favorable to the United States'' mentioned in the ''Defense Guidance'' plan has been replaced by the less provocative ''denying victory to the Soviet Union.'' Draper then accuses Weinberger of both ''denying the aim to 'prevail' and affirming the plan to prevail.'' Weinberger, in a final letter, seems to have little to say in rebuttal of this point. He writes that American military policy as a whole is ''defensive,'' as though Draper had accused the Administration of planning aggression (he had not), and then, once more addressing the crucial question of what the American plan should be if deterrence fails, merely comes up with a slightly milder and even more euphemistic version of his previous answer. This time, he says that the United States should seek to "terminate the conflict quickly at the lowest level of destruction possible, to restore deterrence, and to protect the sovereignty and continued viability of the United States and of the Western democracies as free societies with fundamental institutions and values intact." But then he shifts from defense of Administration policies to criticism of the policy supported by Draper, who believes that the United States should possess enough nuclear forces to annihilate the Soviet Union in a retaliatory strike and then stop. "Although . . . you believe massive response against the Soviet population is the response necessary to provide for deterrence, for political, military, and yes, moral reasons, we do not target civilian populations as such," Weinberger writes. "If we are forced to retaliate and can only respond by destroying population centers, we invite the destruction of our own population. Such a deterrent strategy could lack conviction, particularly as a deterrent to nuclear—let alone conventional—attack on an ally." In other words, he articulates the nuclear-warfighters' complaint against mutual assured destruction: that suicide is not a very plausible threat.

Now it is Draper's turn to lack an answer. In fact, in his next letter he fails to take up the question of what he proposes that the United States should do if deterrence breaks down; instead he concentrates more fire on Weinberger's unconvincing answers to the same question. Weinberger's charge that to unleash mutual assured destruction is senseless as an action and implausible as a threat is permitted to stand. In short, in responding (or, in Draper's case, failing to respond) to the question of what to do "if deterrence fails," each man succeeds in demonstrating the senselessness of the other man's plan and does not succeed in defending his own plan. It's a case of mutual assured destruction. And both are right. Draper succeeds in showing that Weinberger really wants to win a nuclear war, and that this hope is utterly illusory, but he cannot find any justification for actually carrying out the mutual assured destruction that he supports. He is reduced to saying, in effect, that deterrence *won't* fail. Thus, in his second letter he says that the only "effective use" of nuclear weapons is to "prevent their use" in the first place. But that answer begs the question under discussion, which is what to do with them *if prevention fails* and nuclear bombs are landing on one's soil. In other words, there is no deterrence without a threat. The question is: Threat of what? As Weinberger points out, the answer given to *this* question by policymakers, *now*, before any attack has been made, theoretically bears on whether prevention itself will work, since under the deterrence doctrine it is fear of retaliation that keeps the first strike from being launched. Weinberger, for his part, succeeds in showing that mutual assured destruction is a senseless action and therefore an unconvincing threat, but he cannot demonstrate that in the nuclear war he apparently has in mind we can actually preserve our "institutions and values intact" or "force" the Soviet Union to accept "terms favorable to the United States," or achieve any of the other things he promises in his long string of euphemisms for victory.

The truth that neither man wants to face up to is that there is nothing that it would make sense to do "if de-

terrence fails"—nothing, that is, but to get on the hot
line and try to stop the whole debacle as soon as possible. But that intention cannot be spelled out in advance by government officials as their "response" to
nuclear attack, because deterrence requires that they
threaten devastating retaliation of one kind or another,
be it attempted nuclear-war-fighting or straight mutual
assured destruction. When the President is asked what
the United States will do if it is subjected to nuclear attack by the Soviet Union, he cannot answer, "I will immediately call up the Soviet Premier and ask him to
please stop." He cannot tell the world that if we suffer
nuclear attack our retaliation will be a phone call. For
the instant he gave that answer deterrence would dissolve. Once again, we arrive at the very core of what is
wrong with deterrence, which can be stated very simply: it commits us in certain circumstances to do what
we must never do in any circumstances—plunge into a
nuclear holocaust, in which our species could be destroyed and the human story ended forever. Deterrence
theory is indeed a marvel of circularity and contradiction. To obtain the benefit of the policy, we must
threaten to perform an insane action. But the benefit we
seek is precisely *not* to perform that action. We thus
seek to avoid performing an act by threatening to perform it. As long as the policy succeeds, of course,
everyone is happy. But the moment it fails we would
like to scrap the whole thing, because then we find ourselves committed to performing an insane action—to
doing the very thing whose avoidance was the purpose
of the policy. But if, looking ahead to this terrible moment, we admit now that once the breakdown occurs
(and Soviet troops are flooding into Western Europe,

for example) we don't want to perform the insane act of shoving the world into the abyss of doom we lose the pre-breakdown benefits that we now enjoy. So we don't admit it—perhaps not even to ourselves—and continue to stand ready to perform the act.

Draper and Weinberger have their separate ways of evading this terrible truth of our time. Draper simply declines to acknowledge the illogic of making a threat whose execution would be senseless. Weinberger, in an apparent step forward, acknowledges the illogic, but then, in his attempt to repair it, takes two steps backward, by taking leave of the reality that gave rise to the whole problem in the first place—the reality of the overwhelming destructive force of the weapons, which are more than a match for any institutions we have, not to speak of "values." (It's when *we* annihilate *them* that our "values" are destroyed.) In effect, he and the Administration he speaks for have escaped from illogic into fantasy. Of the two defects, the illogic, as I have noted, is preferable, in part because it is compensated for by the "existential" qualities of the arsenals, including the impenetrable uncertainty that, in the real world, must reside in the minds of all sensible people regarding what would happen once a nuclear holocaust actually started. If there must be nuclear weapons, then this uncertainty, and not the iron resolve to annihilate the adversary and suffer annihilation oneself, in mutual assured destruction, or the supposed ability to defeat him in a "nuclear war," is the strongest buttress of such stability as our jeopardized world now enjoys. The necessity of relying on uncertainty, however—on our *in*ability to control or predict our actions—is only one more demonstration that there is no truly rational or humanly justifiable way either to use or the threaten to use nuclear weapons, and that only their abolition can return our lives to sanity and normality.

In 1946, Bernard Brodie and a number of other strategic thinkers devised the doctrine of deterrence as a means of gaining time for the world while it worked on a true solution to the nuclear problem. But the world, instead of using the time won in this way, chose to forget the underlying issues and to elevate the temporary expedient into a dogma. An improvisation became orthodoxy. Meanwhile, the world, lulled into a false sense of reassurance, in effect went to sleep. In the decades following the invention of the bomb, the doctrine of deterrence achieved a seemingly unchallengeable dominance. Its triumphant progress perhaps reached its apogee in the early 1970s, when the first nuclear-arms-control agreements between the United States and the Soviet Union were signed. So widely accepted in our country had the doctrine become that some likened it to a religious faith, and referred to its experts as a "priesthood"—a priesthood that might argue back and forth in specialized journals over the fine points of theology but was united on the basic articles of the faith. It even had its paradoxes and mysteries (such as what to do if deterrence failed)—an essential ingredient in any theology worth the name. And when the arms-control agreements were signed it seemed that the faith had spread from Washington to Moscow. If all this was "élitist," it was also reassuring. A doctrine was in place that promised "stability" in the world. The two great nuclear adversaries seemed to subscribe to it. (The sheer fact of agreement on *something* was important.) What was better, under its guidance they had reached agreements that promised to be only the first in a long series—a series in which the weapons would be, if not abolished, at least "managed." The direction the two powers were moving in seemed to be the right one. And yet within a few years this solid-seeming edifice had disintegrated. The doctrine of deterrence on which it was based had come apart, the priesthood was scattered, the arms-control "process" was at a standstill, the two great nuclear powers were exchanging insulting and menacing remarks, and the arms race, unguided now by any coherent philosophy on either side—much less by one shared by the two sides—was spiralling out of control.

Deterrence had not been assailed from without. No enemy had challenged it. No consistent new doctrine had taken its place in men's minds. ("Nuclear-war-fighting" remained an uncertain and ambivalent mishmash of atavistic military impulses and abstruse theorizing presented in the teeth of the most elementary facts of the nuclear age.) Rather, deterrence was unraveling from within; it was a victim of its own contradictions, which were seized upon in large measure by its own practitioners. Yet when the contradictions were looked at unblinkingly it turned out that they were inherent in the existence of the doomsday machine itself. For the truth was that there was nothing wrong with the doctrine of deterrence which was not wrong simply with the possession of vast nuclear arsenals—with or without the doctrine of deterrence. The reason that no repair of the doctrine was possible was that the problem did not lie in doctrine. It lay in the world's possession of nuclear arsenals—in their "existential" features, if you like. For, whatever government spokesmen might say about possessing nuclear weapons only to prevent their use, the inescapable truth was that possession inevitably implied use, and use irredeemably senseless, since it threatened to bring about the destruction of whatever one might think one was trying to defend: if you tried to reject deterrence while holding on to the weapons, you only wound up with nuclear-war-fighting. Thus, at bottom, the crisis in doctrine stemmed from the reliance on nuclear arms. Indeed, deterrence was probably the least obnoxious and most sensible doctrine consistent with the absurd situation of processing the arsenals. Most important, it was based on an acknowledgment of the true extent of the peril. Furthermore, it renounced the aggressive use of the weapons, and sought stability rather than military advantages from them. It endeavored to increase the element of *threat* to the maximum while reducing the risk of *use* to the minimum. If this effort was self-contradictory—since the threat was credible only insofar as use was a real possibility—and was in that sense like trying to make use of the shadow of an object without having the object itself, it was certainly better than imagining that after a nuclear holocaust we would wind up with our societies and ''values'' intact.

It was against this background of official confusion and international discord that the new peace movement arose. But while the movement may have been triggered in part by the crisis in the deterrence doctrine it has not taken the restoration of deterrence as its goal. To be sure, some members of the old nuclear priesthood have come to the defense of their beleaguered doctrine, but only to find real priests challenging it, in the bishops' pastoral letter. It turned out that while the nuclear-war-fighters were looking at the contradictions of deterrence and worrying about the loss of credibility people on the outside were looking at those same contradictions and worrying about the loss of mankind itself. Having made their conscious choice in favor of human survival, they could hardly be content with a policy that left mankind perched on the edge of doom and prescribed that in certain not altogether unlikely circumstances we jump. And when the proponents of deterrence began to present the arrangement as permanent, and to rule out full nuclear disarmament even in the long run, the doctrine came to seem an abomination. It began to look like a death sentence for the human race. Yet while extreme dissatisfaction with deterrence was implicit in making the "conscious choice" to try to preserve the human species a critique of deterrence was not yet a deliberate policy of the peace movement.

The world was awakening, but what it was awakening *to* was not a ready solution to the nuclear predicament but, rather, the impasse that the world had reached in the first years of the nuclear age. When the world woke up, it was therefore only to find itself manacled to the bed on which it was lying, for the "impossibility" of any real relief from the nuclear peril—and the impossibility, in particular, of the abolition of nuclear weapons—had been affirmed by decades of strategic thinking. It was perhaps not surprising, then, that many people wanted to go back to sleep—in effect, saying, "Wake us up again when you have some answers." For trailing after the elemental human questions raised by the peace movement was a whole new set of questions, concerning what should be done. Can the goal of a nuclear-free world actually be reached, or is it in fact impossible—a "fictional utopia," as *Living with Nuclear Weapons* tells us? If the Harvard book is right, what then is the outlook? If it is wrong, and the path is open, what then is the path? Is it unilateral disarmament? If so, what would happen to our independence and our liberties? Or is bilateralism best? If it is, how can we in the West, including both governments and the peace movement, bring our influence to bear on the Soviet Union, where no independent peace movement is permitted? Must political détente precede disarmament? If the superpowers are to get rid of half of their weapons, must they first get rid of half of their political differences? Or can disarmament go ahead with political differences intact? If so, how far can it go? *Can* they get rid of half of the weapons? Three-quarters? All? Does world government then become necessary? Or will something else do? In addressing these questions, the peace movement finds itself up against the issues that divided Einstein and Brodie; and the old debate on these issues, which has been in abeyance for some time, has been resumed.

Much of it is the same as in 1945. Once again, supposed "realists" tilt against supposed "idealists"; once again, moralists call strategists immoral, and strategists call moralists naïve; once again, the necessary is called impossible, and the impossible is called necessary. In short, rhetorical warfare has broken out afresh along the whole front of the still unbridged divide that the invention of nuclear weapons opened between the world's historical political organization of human life and human life itself. Yet there are some changes in the debate. Perhaps the most significant change is that the political program of the peace movement, in contrast to that of Einstein and his school, has so far been modest and tentative. There is little appetite for sweeping proposals that might resolve the predicament all at once if they were acted upon but that probably would not be acted upon, because they would be unlikely to meet with official or public acceptance. In particular, there are virtually no new calls for world government—a pair of words so thoroughly out of fashion that merely uttering them seems guaranteed to sink in political oblivion any plan connected with them. For Einstein, the boundlessness of the peril of extinction and the sweeping, radical solution of world government were so tightly connected as to be almost two parts of one thought, with the latter simply implicit in the former. For the peace movement of the 1980s, however, the question has been broken into many thoughts, and there has been a sense of a great distance to be crossed, intellectually as well as politically, between an analysis of the problem and an analysis of its resolution. This dissection of the issue—this opening up of its moral and political dimensions, revealing a richer complexity than had previously been recognized—is probably one more result of the world's years of experience of living with the doomsday machine. In 1945, the peril was on the horizon and was approaching quickly, yet it remained distant and abstract. The bombings of Hiroshima and Nagasaki were soon seen as part of a war that was over, not as harbingers of everybody's future. In 1984, the peril, while still in a sense invisible and abstract, nevertheless surrounds and pervades our lives. It is the sky overhead and the ground underfoot. We are immersed in it and permeated by it. In sum, we now live in a *nuclear world*, and our reactions, our thoughts and feelings, conscious and unconscious, have reference to that world. They have a flavor of experience, which the reactions of people in 1945 could not have.

The American bishop's pastoral letter exemplifies both the spirit and the substance of the new movement. It subjects the nuclear policies of the great powers to searching moral and intellectual scrutiny. The question that the bishops start by asking is not so much "What shall we do?" as the more uncomfortable, prior question "What are we doing?" Though their goal is not novelty—they hold established policies up to the light of time-honored standards and principles—their investigation breaks new ground, for hitherto as a society we have permitted our nuclear policies to escape such examination. By insisting that our political and military practices be judged according to traditional ethical standards, the bishops are taking the first step toward making our sundered world whole. This is a fitting effort for the Catholic Church, which over the centuries has made an effort to find and apply moral standards that are appropriate to all domains of life, public and private. Invoking the just-war theory of Catholic teaching, which says that it is at times permissible to kill in defense of one's country, the bishops sanction the existence of a breach of some size between the moral standards for private conduct and the moral standards for governmental conduct. But they draw limits. First, they declare that nuclear weapons must *never* be used against cities. Quoting the Second Vatican Council, they state, "Any act of war aimed indiscriminately at the destruction of entire cities or of extensive areas along with their population is a crime against God and man himself. It merits unequivocal and unhesitating condemnation." Second, they condemn the initiation of nuclear war, finding it "not justified by rational political objectives." Third, they reject the notion of "limited" nuclear war, stating that to cross the nuclear threshold is "to enter a world where we have no experience of control, much testimony against [limited war's] possibility, and therefore no moral justification for submitting the human community to this risk."

Having made these firm and far-reaching moral judgments, the bishops do not go on to make equally firm and far-reaching recommendations for action on the basis of them. Rather, they subscribe to such moderate and partial proposals as the nuclear freeze and no first use. Like the peace movement as a whole, the bishops are diagnostic radicals but prescriptive moderates. They reserve judgment on the deeper political questions, perhaps because they believe (as I do) that it is only on the prior foundation of a solid moral and intellectual understanding of the predicament that a sound political solution can be built. According to this line of thinking, the present system of deterrence, while possessing virtues that should not be overlooked, is a perfect example of a solution built on shaky foundations, and its recent disarray, which is due more to internal disintegration than to assault from without, is a symptom of its basic infirmity. Seen in this light, the political hesitancy of the bishops and of the movement as a whole must be judged a strength, not a weakness. It bespeaks a wise open-mindedness, not a fatal impracticality or a neglect of the realities of political life. It means only that the bishops are addressing the issue in the two stages recommended by the Pope: first the "conscious choice," then the "deliberate policy." Before the nuclear question could be re-answered, it had to be re-opened, and they have reopened it. However, if those who have raised the question withhold judgment on the policy question for a prolonged period the strength will become a fatal weakness. Beyond a certain point, a failure to follow up the choice with a policy will breed discouragement. The peace movement, like the world as a whole, is in need of proposals for action which are commensurate with the hopes that it has raised, and are answerable to the moral standards it uses to measure present policies. If no such proposals are forthcoming, the peace movement seems sure to dissipate, just as peace movements in the past have dissipated. In that event, a yet more profound atmosphere of fatalism than people have felt so far seems likely to descend over the world, because people will be convinced that even popular action—previously their one untried hope—is helpless in the face of the nuclear peril, which will then truly take on the final aspect of a doomsday machine: something that has been made by human beings but has slipped beyond human control.

For the time being, the movement has given its backing to proposals that are somewhat more ambitious than those normally considered feasible by the arms-control experts but are still moderate enough to win widespread approval. In the United States, the outstanding proposal of this kind is, of course, the freeze, which from the moment it became widely known enjoyed broad public support. (In Europe, the comparable effort, which has now failed, was to block deployment of the Euromissiles.) In fact, the freeze proposal was adopted by the movement perhaps as much for its political "salability" as for its merits, which I believe are nevertheless great. The freeze answers the urgent need to head off the next advance in the arms race, which promises to be a particularly perilous one. The first-strike weapons already deployed by the Soviet Union and the United States have undermined stability, and the weapons planned for the near future—weapons such as the MX and the Trident D-5 missile—would undermine it further. Another peril to stability is the plan to put arms in space, by developing both anti-satellite weapons and space-based anti-missile weapons. Anti-satellite weapons are destabilizing because they threaten to blind the warning systems and the intelligence-gathering systems of one or both sides in a crisis, and leave the statesmen acting in the dark as nuclear hostilities begin. Space-based anti-missile weapons are destabilizing because they could menace the retaliatory capacity of the other side—a threat that would certainly be met either by a further buildup of missiles or by the development of still other weapons, designed to attack the space-based anti-missile ones, or by both. Still another technical development that threatens stability is the cruise missile, which promises to greatly complicate future arms-control talks. Unlike most ballistic missiles, which are large and relatively easy to spot by satellite, cruise missiles are small—as little as eighteen feet long and twenty-one inches in diameter—and therefore easy to conceal. Moreover, cruise missiles, whose eventual deployment may be in the tens of thousands, can be equipped with either nuclear or conventional warheads, and a rival power cannot always know from the outside which is which. Both this difficulty in determining which of them are nuclear-armed and the ease with which they can be hidden would make the verification of arms-control agreements incomparably more complicated than it is today.

While the freeze is fully defensible as a measure in its own right, virtually none of the advocates of the freeze (or of any of the other moderate measures that have been put forward by the peace movement) present it (or any of the others) as the final goal of their efforts. They are well aware that, as an answer to the question of what mankind should do about the threat of human extinction by nuclear arms, the proposal that one should freeze the doomsday machine in place would, if it were to be offered without promise of a further proposal, be a non sequitur. They all, therefore, regard it as only "a first step." A step, however, implies a direction, and a direction implies a goal. Neither the direction nor the goal has yet been defined. If one asks what "the next step" should be, the answer is very likely to be "reductions," or "deep reductions." But when one asks how far the reductions should go, and what sort of world they would lead to, haziness and ambiguity set in. The goal of complete nuclear disarmament is sometimes mentioned, but in a perfunctory, almost casual way. Few details are offered, and no convincing picture of a nuclear-free world has yet been presented.

These lacks are only part of another lack—the lack of any doctrine that could guide the steps toward the goal of complete nuclear disarmament. A doctrine is a comprehensive policy—or, if you like, a "deliberate policy"—for dealing with an entire issue. It offers both a broad picture of the world and long-term goals to strive toward, so that the short-term measures are not a groping in a void, and do not contradict one another. When the issue is nuclear disarmament, the basic question that a doctrine must address is the underlying political one of how, in a world in which war has become mutual annihilation, the bitterest and most intractable disputes among nations are to be settled. In other words, the issue is nothing less than how the world is to be organized politically. Deterrence deserves to be called a doctrine because it offers an answer—however unsatisfactory one may find it—to the political question. It holds that the disputes among nations which in the past have been resolved through war must now be averted by the maintenance of a balance of terror with huge nuclear arsenals. It invites us to tolerate a degree of risk of extinction as the price for national defense and international stability. The proposal for world government, too, deserves to be called a doctrine, because it also answers the basic question—holding that these disputes must be resolved by civil procedures under a global authority. This solution invites us to revolutionize the politics of the earth as the cost of lifting the peril of extinction. Whatever one thinks of the bargain struck by either of these resolutions of the nuclear predicament, both deserve to be recognized as politically ''serious,'' in the sense that both face the basic political issue without evasion. There have, by contrast, been any number of suggestions that have lacked seriousness in this sense. They may, for example, call for nuclear disarmament, or for total disarmament, but without acknowledging the need for the vast political changes that would enable nations to resolve their disputes bindingly by peaceful means and without specifying any such means. Sometimes the intent behind such incomplete proposals may be purely rhetorical, as when a politician wishes to end his speech with an uplifting thought, and sometimes genuine political naïveté may be responsible. Inasmuch as the settlement of the disputes that arise among men is of the very essence of politics, these proposals are truly—to use a much-abused term—politically "unrealistic." They simply evade the political dimension of the issue altogether.

So far, the current peace movement has not given any significant backing to proposals that ignore the political dimension of the predicament. Rather, to the extent that it has recommended actions it has largely insisted on political workability throughout, and has chosen the course of backing modest but useful plans of action, such as the freeze within the framework of existing broad policy, and of leaving the deeper political question open for the time being. Uneasy with deterrence but uninterested in world government, the peace movement seeks to chart a new course, but it has not yet found a way to do it. Lacking any doctrine to call its own, the movement has been driven reluctantly to rely for now on the basic framework of deterrence to justify its moderate proposals. Thus, it defends the freeze in part on the ground that it will stabilize deterrence, and protect the nuclear balance from the technical developments that threaten to destabilize it in the near future. And, in fact, the acceptability of the freeze is probably attributable in no small measure to its compatibility with deterrence. (A recent poll showed that seventy per cent of the American public favored a freeze.) Accordingly, in putting forward the freeze the peace movement offers the world a new step to take but borrows an old doctrine to justify it. This borrowing is in itself unexceptionable (since it is a clear benefit to everybody for the present system to be made safer and for future deterioration of its stability to be headed off), but it has a high price attached if it continues for very long. For the premise of the doctrine of deterrence—that safety can be maintained only by the maintenance of large nuclear arsenals—is at odds with the deepest premise of the new movement, which is that we must somehow stop threatening ourselves with annihilation. The bishops' pastoral letter can again serve as an illustration.

The bishops begin by unequivocally condemning the mass slaughter of innocents with nuclear weapons. Yet deterrence requires such slaughter—or, at the very least, cannot promise to avoid it—simply because any large-scale nuclear attack, even if it is aimed at military targets, will involve the mass slaughter of innocents. There is, of course, a policy that would succeed in translating the pastoral letter's ban on nuclear mass slaughter into actual policy. It is unilateral disarmament—and not some unilateral "gesture" or other but the real thing: an immediate declaration by the President that he was dismantling the nation's nuclear arsenal in the shortest possible time, and that meanwhile he renounced the use of nuclear weapons. Yet if there are two words that in the present political climate doom a proposal to political oblivion even more swiftly than "world government" they are "unilateral disarmament," and the bishops explicitly reject this course. Nevertheless, they seem at times to steer in its direction. At one point in the letter, they observe that "the political paradox of deterrence has also strained our moral conception.'' Then they pose a series of questions: ''May a nation threaten what it may never do? May it possess what it may never use? Who is involved in the threat each superpower makes: Government officials? Or military personnel? Or the citizenry in whose defense the threat is made?'' This series of questions has the look of an exploratory probe of dangerous territory—a probe in which the bishops reconnoitre the perilous ground of unilateral disarmament only to veer away again. For if these questions are answered in a certain way they make the moral argument for unilateral nuclear disarmament: ''A nation may never threaten what it may never do. It must never possess what it may never use. Not only government officials and military personnel but also the citizenry in whose defense the threat is made are involved in the threat.'' Judged by traditional ethical standards, including, specifically, the Catholic teaching on war, this position is not an extreme one. It does not rule out all killing, for example. It does not even rule out killing on quite a large scale. It merely spells out the measures necessary if the injunction against the mass slaughter of innocents is to be more than exhortation and become policy. The bishops boldly ask us whether we are willing, under any conceivable circumstances, to kill countless millions of innocent people, and to this their and our immediate impulse is to cry out ''No!'' And, indeed, at one point the bishops state that we must say a clear ''no'' to nuclear weapons. If I may use myself as an example, I know that if the nuclear button were on my desk and a nuclear attack were launched against the United States I would be unable to retaliate in kind. I would utterly lack the "resolve" to do this. In fact, my whole resolve would be that it not be done. This 'retaliation" would seem to me to be a separate, new unspeakable crime in its own right, which was in no way an appropriate response to the unspeakable crime that had just been committed against my country. As I see it, it would, in fact, not even *be* retaliation, since most of the people it would kill—innocent citizens, including children—would have had nothing to do with their government's criminally insane decision. Yet I know that this unwillingness of mine would, if it were generalized into a policy, be so far outside the pale politically as to have virtually no acceptance. In that sense, to truly say "no" to nuclear weapons forces one into a position that is politically irrelevant—at least, as far as present policy is concerned. Although I can't speak for others, I suspect that there are many people who want to say a real "no" to nuclear weapons but find that majority opinion is overwhelmingly against them. So, in desperation, they, like the bishops, seek partial and gradual measures that, if they are pursued long enough, may enable us one day not only to say but to practice our "no."

The fissure that nuclear weapons have created between our political selves and our moral selves is precisely delineated by the fact that as long as there are nuclear weapons in the world we are compelled to choose between a position that is politically sound but immoral and one that is morally sound but politically irrelevant. The bishops, who have had the rare courage to articulate the dilemma, oscillate between these two positions and conclude with a compromise. Having begun by condemning the slaughter of innocents with nuclear arms, they appear to catch a glimpse of the political implication of that stand (unilateral disarmament) and reject it, and finally fall back on deterrence, to which they give a "strictly conditioned" acceptance—the condition being that deterrence be recognized as a provisional remedy while full-scale nuclear disarmament is being worked out. (On this point, I find myself in disagreement with the bishops. My unwillingness to support the use or the threat to use nuclear weapons is unconditional. There are simply some means that I think are wrong, no matter what the end pursued, and this is one of them. And if it is wrong in that sense, then it is wrong in all times and places and circumstances, including now, right here, and in our present circumstances. If we are attacked with nuclear weapons, I *want* the retaliation to be a phone call. Thus, unlike the bishops, I cannot support deterrence conditionally, because I think that it is as wrong conditionally as it is eternally, If, while awaiting a full solution to the nuclear problem, we, in obedience to the dictates of deterrence policy, take action that leads to the death of billions of people, they will not be conditionally dead. And if we extinguish mankind it will not be conditionally extinguished. It will be extinguished forever. At the same time, however, precisely because extinction is forever, I believe that moderate steps that fall short of a full solution to the nuclear peril should receive everyone's wholehearted support. We can and must morally boycott evil in this world, but we cannot boycott the world. The purity of an individual person's conduct has immeasurable importance for *the world*. But if in seeking to preserve our purity we let *the world* perish, of what use will our purity be then?) The bishops state that we must say a clear "no" to nuclear

weapons. Ultimately, however, their "no" is qualified, and nuclear weapons are accepted, if only tem-
porarily. The bishops articulate the soul's demand that
we desist at all costs from carrying out mass murder and
the extinction of our species, but they do not find a home
for that demand in our present world. Yet the choked-
back "no" continues to sound beneath the argumen-
tation and compromise. It becomes the banked moral
fire that is needed to keep the idea of disarmament active in our thoughts and efforts.

The bishops' U-turn, in which they criticize but then
embrace deterrence, although only provisionally and
with barely contained revulsion, reflects the whole
peace movement's rejection of the premises of deterrence and its simultaneous reliance on deterrence to justify the moderate and politically popular proposals that
it has put forward. Moral and intellectual torment, of
which the pastoral letter is a paradigm, is one of the results of that reliance. Another, which has greater practical consequences, is that of leaving the movement
without any road map to full nuclear disarmament to offer the world—and, worse, we are all left to rely on a
road map that specifically precludes full nuclear disarmament. For while the people of the peace movement
have not examined in detail the possibility of nuclear
disarmament in the framework of deterrence, the theorists of deterrence have, and they have all but unani-
mously ruled it out as unattainable—as "a fictional
utopia."

The popular notion of a whole series of "steps,"
which evokes the image of a stairway, encourages the
simple but hopeful idea that if enough steps are taken

the top of the stairway will be reached and complete nuclear disarmament will be attained. And certainly the usefulness of distinguishing between short-term steps and long-term goals seems obvious and undeniable. It needs to be said—once and for all, one would hope—that there is no need whatever to choose between short-term, moderate ''steps'' that are within our immediate grasp and long-term, radical goals whose achievement would bring us real safety. Nothing is more arid and fruitless than the abuse-laden exchanges between the champions of these two approaches, with one side saying that the moderate steps are useless because they don't go far enough, and the other side saying that long-term goals should be barred from the discussion because they will distract us from moderate measures that we can really achieve. These arguments are like the wasted breath of two people standing at the bottom of a stairway arguing about whether it is more important to take the first step or the last step to get to the top. Isn't it self-evident that both are needed? The two camps would do well to call a cease-fire and become allies, with the short-term people gaining hope and a sense of direction from a new understanding that long-term goals are both essential and achievable, and the long-term people taking heart from the actual accomplishments of the short-term people. And then, of course, they could pit their combined efforts against the steady retrogression that has been our real record over the last thirty-nine years.

However, an agreement on the obvious point that all the steps—first, middle, and last—must be traversed if one is to get to the top of the stairs would hardly solve the substantive question of just *which* stairway leads to safety (if such a thing is attainable at all in the nuclear world). Close examination of the doctrine of deterrence dashes the hope that *this* doctrine is such a stairway. The problem is inherent in the very nature of deterrence as it is currently practiced. Under deterrence, "safety" lies in the weapons themselves, and in the terror they inspire. More particularly, it lies in the power of each side to destroy the society of the other side after suffering a first strike. If that power is lost, then the balance of terror is lost, and deterrence dissolves. Deterrence thus establishes a level beneath which "reductions" may not go, and the level is the number of weapons necessary to destroy the society of the adversary in a retaliatory strike. This situation is often called "minimum deterrence," and it marks the lower limits of arms reductions under the doctrine of deterrence in its present form. Under deterrence, arms control can theoretically eliminate redundancy, but it must never touch the essential capacity for "assuring" the annihilation of the other side. In other words, it can get rid of the overkill but not the kill—an advance, but not one that offers much relief to people in the targeted countries. Indeed, in the light of the conclusion that even a fraction of the present arsenals could trigger a nuclear winter, it turns out that there might not even be any relief for untargeted nations, whose interests might otherwise be served by a policy of minimum deterrence. From the point of view of a mortal human being, the first time you lose your life is the time that counts, and whether or not your ghost is being stalked through the rubble by further nuclear explosions is a point of small interest. Another problem with minimum deterrence, which was seized on by Weinberger in his argument with Draper (who, however, favors not "minimum" but what he calls "sufficient" deterrence), is that it leaves the statesmen with an all-or-nothing choice as soon as the brink is reached, and deprives them of all flexibility.

Reduction to zero is, of course, ruled out. For, according to the terms of the doctrine, if nations had no nuclear weapons to threaten one another with, deterrence would evaporate. In fact, there is a sense in which even reductions are antithetical to the logic of deterrence: if under this doctrine safety relies on terror, then it may be dangerous—destabilizing—to undermine, or even to "minimize," that terror, because one might at the same time minimize the safety. The only reason to minimize the number of weapons would be to minimize the damage "if deterrence fails," but such minimizing runs directly counter to the essence of the logic of deterrence, which is that everyone will be dissuaded from launching an attack only because everyone knows that the damage to his own society will be the maximum possible. It can even be argued that overkill is useful in producing a deterrent effect. It may eliminate every last shred of doubt on either side that to make war in a nuclear world is to commit suicide. (And the recent statements by our own government officials show how durable the illusion is that one might survive—or even come out on top—in a nuclear war.)

A goal for arms control which does make sense under the doctrine of deterrence is stability, but stability is not necessarily served by reductions; rather, increases to assure "the survivability of the retaliatory force," for example, or to heighten that force's destructive power might in some circumstances be judged necessary. In fact, a minor argument has broken out in the arms-control world between the advocates of reductions and the advocates of stabilization. The former aim at reducing the numbers of nuclear weapons, apparently in the hope that the momentum achieved might lead the world to safety. The latter argue that, given the existence of nuclear arsenals, the numbers are unimportant, and the thing to do is to remove the technical imbalances and the political tensions that could lead to use of the arsenals—whatever their size. (The ultimate stabilization, of course, would be for the Soviet Union and the United States to come to an understanding regarding their international differences.) However, both schools accept the underlying framework of deterrence. Deterrence is a system—a way of organizing the nuclear world. As such, it has an underlying logic (though a flawed one), definite rules and provisions, and definite military and technical requirements. If in order to achieve the abolition, or even the severe reduction, of nuclear weapons this logic is to be abandoned, its rules broken, and its provisions violated, then some other system—some other way of organizing the world—has to be offered in its stead.

The theorists of deterrence do not altogether rule out the abolition of nuclear weapons; they rule it out only as a measure that is possible in a word of sovereign states. If we are to achieve the abolition of nuclear weapons—not to mention complete disarmament—then, they say, we must establish world government. World government, they admit, could at least theoretically replace deterrence. But they reject world government, and with it, abolition. According to this view, we must choose between a nuclear-armed world of sovereign states and a nuclear-free world ruled by world government. The one thing they see as truly impossible, in the long run as well as the short run, is a world of still sovereign states from which nuclear weapons have been abolished. This is because they see no way that the political question—how disputes among nations are to be resolved—can be answered in such a world. They foresee that if in such a world a dispute arises and diplomatic efforts are unavailing, then one or both countries will shortly rearm and war will break out. What is worse, in anticipation of such a conflict some nations may secretly stockpile or actually produce nuclear weapons, in undetectable violation of the abolition agreement, so as to have an immediate and overwhelming advantage over their potential adversaries—or, at any rate, to avoid being left at a hopeless disadvantage if it turns out that the adversary has cheated. And the deterrence theorists note, as a clinching argument, that even if it should happen that no one was violating the agreement the knowledge of how to make the weapons would remain in the world, and nations could rebuild nuclear weapons openly as soon as some unresolvable political dispute broke out. Since in this view political disputes are sooner or later inevitable, it would not be long before the whole world had embarked again on a chaotic, pell-mell nuclear-arms race—the worst of all possible results. This line of thinking, though it is no secret, is not widely known among the public, yet among strategic analysts it is broadly accepted. And since it is to the analysts, by and large, that the politicians turn when they wish to translate hopeful rhetoric into action this view stands as a serious obstacle to any plan for full nuclear disarmament—and should so stand unless the points made can be answered. The following are but a few examples of this reasoning. Herman Kahn wrote in 1960:

> It has probably always been impractical to imagine a completely disarmed world, and the introduction of the thermonuclear bomb has added a special dimension to this impracticality. Given the large nuclear stockpiles in the Soviet Union, the United States, and the British Isles, it would be child's play for one of these nations to hide completely hundreds of these bombs. . . . The violator would then have an incredible advantage if the agreement ever broke down and the arms race started again. This surely means that even if all nations should one day agree to total nuclear disarmament, we must presume that there would be the hiding of some nuclear weapons or components as a hedge against the other side doing so. An international arrangement for banishing war through disarmament will not call for total disarmament but will almost undoubtedly include provisions for enforcement that cannot be successfully overturned by a small hidden force. Otherwise it would be hopelessly unstable. . . .
>
> While total disarmament can be ruled out as an immediate possibility, one can conceive of some sort of international authority which might have a monopoly of war-making capability. . . . However, it is most doubtful in the absence of a crisis or war that a world government can be set up in the next decade.

Living with Nuclear Weapons makes some of these same points:

> Complete disarmament would require some form of world government to deter actions of one nation against another. In a disarmed world, without such a government armed with sufficient force to prevent conflict between or among nations, differences in beliefs and interests might easily lead to a renewal of war. But any world government capable of preventing world conflict could also become a world dictatorship. And given the differences in ideology, wealth, and nationalism that now exist in the world, most states are not likely to accept a centralized government unless they feel sure of controlling it or minimizing its intrusiveness.

And the M.I.T. political scientist and arms-control expert George Rathjens, in an essay published in 1977 in which he advocates large reductions in the nuclear arsenals of both sides, writes:

> We reject the possibility of complete nuclear disarmament as being unrealistic for the foreseeable future. This becomes clear as soon as one faces up to the changes in the political environment that would be required. . . .
> (a) All states would have to be parties to disarmament agreement. . . .
> (b) All would have to accept such intrusive inspection as to preclude weapons manufacture. . . .

(c) To be sure of timely access to any suspected installation where nuclear weapons might be stored or produced, the forces available to the international authority would have to be sufficiently strong to overcome resistance rapidly. . . .

We are, then, for all practical purposes, dealing with the question of the establishment of a world government (or something very close to it), and one with rather extraordinary powers of search and seizure at that.

As it happens, agreement on this point extends even to the advocates of world government. Both see an unbreakable linkage between full nuclear (or total) disarmament and world government. In *World Peace Through World Law*, published in 1958, which is one of the most carefully thought through of the proposals for world government, Grenville Clark and Louis B. Sohn spell out the minimum that they think would be necessary:

Apart from an effective inspection system to supervise the disarmament process from the outset, it will be indispensable simultaneously to establish an adequate world police force in order that, after complete disarmament has been accomplished, the means will exist to deter or apprehend violators of the world law forbidding any national armaments and prohibiting violence or the threat of it between nations. It will then become equally clear that along with the prohibition of violence or the threat of it as the means of dealing with international disputes, it will be essential to establish alternative peaceful means to deal with all disputes between nations in the shape of a world judicial and conciliation system. It will doubtless also be found advisable, in the interest of a solid and durable peace, to include a World Development Authority, adequately and reliably financed, in order to mitigate the vast disparities between the "have" and the "have not" nations.

The necessity will also be seen for a world legislature with carefully limited yet adequate powers. . . . In addition, it will be necessary to constitute an effective world executive, free from any crippling veto, in order to direct and control the world inspection service and the world police force and to exercise other essential executive functions. Finally, it will follow as surely as day follows night that an effective world revenue system must be adopted.

And, in 1955, Bertrand Russell wrote:

It would be wholly futile to get an agreement prohibiting the H-Bomb. Such an agreement would not be considered binding after war has broken out, and each side on the outbreak of war would set to work to manufacture as many bombs as possible.

I might add that in *The Fate of the Earth* (in which I sought to define the political task posed by nuclear weapons but did not propose any course of action) I wrote:

This task [of resolving the nuclear predicament] falls into two parts—two aims. The first is to save the world from extinction by eliminating nuclear weapons from the earth. . . . The second aim, which alone can provide a sure foundation for the first, is to create a political means by which the world can arrive at the decisions that sovereign states previously arrived at through war. These two aims . . . are intimately connected. If, on the one hand, disarmament is not accompanied by a political solution, then every clash of will between nations will tempt them to pick up the instruments of violence again, and so lead the world back toward extinction. If, on the other hand, a political solution is not accompanied by complete disarmament, then the political decisions that are made will not be binding, for they will be subject to challenge by force.

(I take the liberty of quoting myself again only because I wish to acknowledge my former adherence to a point of view with which I now propose to argue.)

These statements, and countless others that might be quoted, form a remarkable consensus. One school favors world government and the other opposes it, yet they agree that if full nuclear disarmament (or total disarmament) is to be achieved world government is necessary. They make different choices, but they agree on what the choices are, and they agree that between the two there is no middle ground. The changeover is from one fundamental organization of the world to another. And each organization has its own logic and fundamental structure, radically different from the other's.

Deterrence, as we have seen, cannot countenance any reductions below what is necessary for "minimum deterrence," and even these reductions, it is sometimes argued, may be destabilizing. But world government, as the passage by Clark and Sohn makes clear, has an even more comprehensive and indivisible logic—one that moves from an inspection force to a police force, and from a police force to a court, so that by the time you reach the end of the paragraph you have a "World Development Authority," set up to hand over the money of the "have" nations to the "have not" nations. The real problem with world government, as this passage suggests, is not that it is "impossible," or "utopian"—for if enough people want it they can surely have it—but that if we choose it we get more than we want. The heart sinks at the thought of world government not because it is "unrealistic" but because it is all too real. To use a homely metaphor, it is like one of those mail-order clubs in which to receive an attractive introductory offer of, say, a book or a plant one must accept for the rest of the year a monthly book or plant that one may not want. We want relief from the nuclear peril, but if we sign up for world government as the means of getting it we find that global institution after global institution is inexorably delivered on our doorstep thereafter, each one equipped to meddle in some new area of our lives. We are caught up, seemingly for purely technical reasons, in a whirlwind of political change that, in and of itself, we do not want. (The reason for what seems the illimitably sweeping character of world government is easier to understand when one recalls that it is being instituted as a replacement for war, which was previously the "final arbiter" of *all* international disputes, no matter what their character or origin might be.) We would like world government to make just one decision—to ''ban'' (as it's often put) nuclear weapons—but we find that in order to do that it must apparently have the power to make almost any decision we can think of. And from this unlimited delegation of power we shrink back. (Most proposals for world government, and particularly those made by Americans or Englishmen, are hedged about with all kinds of restraints, but, while the restraints might indeed work and be useful, experience tells us that they can always break down, and it is hard to place much trust in them.)

In sum, I am suggesting that the reason we have failed to achieve nuclear disarmament in the last thirty-nine years is not merely that we have lacked the fortitude or the will or the moral sensitivity (although we can hardly exonerate ourselves on those counts) but also that even on the purely intellectual level we have been missing a piece of the puzzle: a way of abolishing nuclear weapons that does not require us to found a world government, which the world shows virtually no interest in founding. The requirement for world government as the inevitable price for nuclear disarmament is at the heart of the impasse that the world has been unable to break through in almost four decades of the nuclear age. It stops citizens and government officials alike from clearly advocating the natural and obvious goal of their anti-nuclear efforts: the abolition of nuclear arms. The linkage is in itself paralyzing. Until it is removed—until we find some way of ridding ourselves of nuclear weapons without having to establish world government, or something like it—major relief from the nuclear peril seems unlikely.

Once the early hopes for a nuclear-free world raised by the advocates of world government had, in the late 1940s, been effectively buried, the tone and content of the continuing discussion of the nuclear question in official circles came to be conditioned by a key piece of reasoning. The reasoning ran: If nuclear weapons are to be abolished, there must be world government; world government is impossible; therefore, we must arm ourselves with nuclear weapons. Once this piece of reasoning was accepted, the greatest of the human and moral questions that were raised by nuclear weapons—questions such as whether it was acceptable to annihilate whole nations, or whether it made sense to build the machinery for the self-extermination of mankind—were, in effect, ruled out of order. For if there was only one path—world government—that led to complete nuclear disarmament, and that path was blocked, a nuclear buildup became inevitable. There is moral responsibility only where there is choice, but here no choice was seen, and therefore no responsibility was seen, either. While the necessity for threatening to use, and perhaps one day actually using, nuclear weapons was certainly regrettable, it was suggested that there was no sense in losing sleep over it until someone showed a plausible way of abolishing them. The remaining questions were details: how many millions you had to threaten to kill to make deterrence take effect, how many bombs you needed to do it, how to keep your retaliatory force safe, etc. The underlying logic constituted a license, which has been honored until the present, to "think the unthinkable" without any qualms.

And if anyone protested the amoral coldness of this thinking, the burden of proof was on him. Did he propose world government? Did he suppose that it could be established and established in time to prevent a nuclear holocaust? Could he point to some other way of abolishing nuclear weapons? If not, it was said, he should hold his tongue.

In 1961, James Newman, an editor on the staff of *Scientific American,* reviewing Herman Kahn's book *On Thermonuclear War* in that periodical, described it as "a moral tract on mass murder: how to plan it, how to commit it, how to get away with it, how to justify it." Kahn's book was exactly that, but so was every book on nuclear strategy—unless it advocated unilateral disarmament—and if Newman could not show the way to avoid this mass murder, then the question was whether he really had the standing to complain. He could be seen to be just as deeply implicated as Kahn was, the only difference being that Kahn was ready to think about the mass murder and talk about it, while Newman was not. (So firmly rooted was the underlying justification for nuclear strategizing that the theorists of the unthinkable at times assumed an air of martyred dignity, as though they were being held in disrepute for volunteering to take up a necessary but painful burden that the rest of society was too weak or squeamish to shoulder. And the theorists were absolutely right—as long as everyone agreed that a nuclear-armed world was the realistic one.)

The new peace movement now finds itself in the same position as James Newman. Its members have exhumed the elemental human and moral questions that are posed by nuclear weapons. They have discovered their revulsion against the idea of enjoying a precarious "safety" at the price of holding hostage the life of every human being on earth and every future, unborn human being. They have awakened with shock and horror to the realization that, like a demented person who has filled the basement of his house with TNT and threatens to set it off, the human family has crammed its planetary home, unmenaced by any outside power, with nuclear weapons. They have rebelled against the belief that mankind's "no" to nuclear slaughter and self-annihilation is untranslatable into action, and must always be blocked by an impenetrable shield of political impossibility. And all this has been essential work, without which mankind would never be able to escape from its self-constructed trap. But now they are asked—and rightly—what plan they have to offer to show the way out of the impasse. If they have none, it is said, they are airing their anguish and indignation before the public for nothing—behavior comparable to running up to someone on death row and shouting "You must die! You must die!" Their challenge, and everyone's challenge, is to unmake the chain of reasoning that locks us in inaction, to break through the shield of political impossibility, and to chart the path that leads back to survival.

II.

A DELIBERATE POLICY

THE CONSENSUS, among so many of those who have thought deeply about the nuclear predicament, that nuclear weapons cannot be abolished unless world government is established seems to find support in traditional political theory: in the distinction between the so-called state of nature, in which men live in anarchy and resolve their disputes among themselves, with war serving as the final arbiter, and the so-called civil state, in which men live under a government and submit their disputes to its final arbitration. In reflecting on the formation of states out of warring tribes or principalities, political thinkers have often observed that the transition from the state of nature to the civil state is usually radical and abrupt, frequently involving some act of conquest or other form of violence, and admits of no partial or halfway solutions, in which, say, a central authority is given the legislative power to "decide" the outcome of disputes but not the executive power to enforce its decisions. We seem to be faced with the same radical, either-or choice in the world as a whole, in which nations, although each constitutes a civil state within its own borders, have, according to the traditional view, always lived in an anarchic state of nature in their relations with each other. The United Nations, which has been helpful in moderating hostilities in our tense and warlike world but has not been empowered to resolve basic disputes among nations, appears to exemplify what halfway measures toward entry into the civil state lead to in the global arena.

The reason that halfway measures toward the civil state never seem to amount to very much is straightforward and basic. Human beings, existing on earth in large numbers and possessed of separate and independent wills, inevitably get into disputes, and government and war are the two immemorial means by which the disputes have been bindingly resolved. Nations do not dare to give up war and disarm until world government, or some equivalent, is in place, because if they did they would be left without any final arbiter for settling disputes. This situation would be inherently unstable, because as soon as a serious dispute arose—concerning, for example, who was to control a certain piece of territory—nations would reach for the instruments of war, and the impotent, halfway civil measures would be ignored or swept aside (as happened, for example, to the League of Nations in the 1930s). That is why the political thinkers of our time have, with rare unanimity, declared that either total disarmament or full nuclear disarmament is impossible without the simultaneous establishment of world government—and we are left with the unfortunate choice between living with a full balance of nuclear terror, which we would like to get away from, and instituting a full global state, which we would like to avoid. (Mere nuclear disarmament is seen as impossible without world government because among the instruments of war nuclear arms overrule all the others. They have the final word.)

The key event is the transition from the state of nature to the civil state is the centralization of power, in which the individual nations (or people) renounce their right to resort to force at their own discretion, yielding it to the central authority, which is then empowered to make and enforce final decisions. Unfortunately, the centralization of power does not necessarily require a shift from "lawlessness" to "law," as advocates of world government sometimes seem to suggest. The central authority can be, in a moral sense, as "lawless" as any individual. When the central authority in question is a world government, this possibility assumes terrifying proportions, which have no precedent in the annals of politics. Moreover, the establishment of a central authority does not necessarily entail a reduction in the levels of violence, as the record of the totalitarian regimes in the first half of our century makes clear (and as the record of the Pol Pot government in Kampuchea has made clear more recently). Governments, we are forced to acknowledge, are fully as capable of slaughtering huge numbers of people as war is. And if a lawless government were to assume control of the world and such slaughter were to be carried out in the global darkness of the oppression of all mankind the horror of the situation would be beyond all imagining.

What the world's entry into the civil state would accomplish, however, is, as everyone acknowledges, an end to war—or, in our time, an end to the possibility of "mutual assured destruction" and human extinction. In war, the level of force used is bid up to the maximum, because victory (if any) goes to the side that keeps on fighting longer. War is, in Clausewitz's words, a form of "reciprocal action" that "must lead to an extreme" in order to reach a conclusion. And for that reason nuclear weapons spoil war as a final arbiter of international disputes: the extreme they run to is total annihilation. Central governments, on the other hand, don't need to run to any extremes of force to carry out even the most extensive slaughter. One bullet for each "subversive," fired into the back of the head, will suffice. In fact, strictly speaking, no active violence at all is necessary. Vast populations can be killed off by simple deprivation. If you place a multitude of people in a camp, force them to work hard, and cut back their rations, you can kill as many of them as you want to. Certainly no nuclear bombs will be necessary to kill them. In that limited, tragic sense, world government, even at its worst, would be a way out of the nuclear predicament. (Of course, if world government were to break down, and civil war were to arise, the nuclear peril might re-arise with it; but just at the moment the peril of a nuclear holocaust resulting from a breakdown of world government is, I should say, the least of our worries.) Even if one regards these worst-case nightmares of world government run amok as unlikely, the prospect of a supreme political power ruling over the whole earth remains chilling. Anarchy is not liberty, yet it could be that in anarchy, with all its violence, the human spirit has greater latitude to live and grow than it would have in the uniform shadow of a global state.

To be sure, for a number of people it is not the attractions of world government that lead them to favor that particular resolution of the nuclear predicament. It is their dismay at what they see as the alternative: an indeterminate period of life on the edge of the abyss, terminated by extinction. The real choice, they say, is not between world government and anarchy but between world government and nothing—"one world or none," as people used to put it. Nevertheless, most people are agreed that the immediate political choice before us is between an anarchic state of nature, in which nations possess nuclear weapons, and the civil state, or world government, in which they would not. (Some people, it is true, have suggested that the world government itself might have to possess nuclear weapons—a prospect that can only increase one's misgivings about this institution.) This definition of the actions open to us is at the heart of an impasse in which the world has been stuck throughout the nuclear age.

In *The Nuclear Revolution: International Politics Before and After Hiroshima,* of 1981, the political scientist Michael Mandelbaum, reflecting the opinion of the consensus—which includes both the advocates of world government and the advocates of our present-day policy of nuclear deterrence—writes, "Relations among sovereign states are still governed by the principle of anarchy. War is still possible." And he goes on:

A logical way to do away with war among nation-states is to abolish national armaments altogether. This, in turn, requires abolishing the incentives for states to have armaments. They have them because of the insecurity that arises from the

123

anarchical structure of the international system. So the requirement for disarmament is the disappearance of anarchy, in favor of an international system organized along the lines of the state in domestic politics. States must give up sovereignty. This is the political revolution that some anticipated in 1945 but that has not come to pass.

In this view, evidently, our world of nuclear-armed deterrence remains in the traditional anarchic state of nature. I should like to argue, however, that inasmuch as nuclear weapons have spoiled war—the final arbiter in the state of nature—we are mistaken about this, having been misled by the habits of pre-nuclear political thought, which so often lead us astray in the new and strange nuclear world. A deterred world, I believe, is no longer in anarchy—in the traditional state of nature. Nor, of course, is it in the civil state. It is not even quite in between the two but, rather, is in a new state altogether—the deterred state—which has been brought into being by the all-pervasive, deeply rooted, man-made reality of a nuclear-capable world. It was, I believe, an unacknowledged change of this kind that Einstein was referring to when he made his famous remark, "The unleashed power of the atom has changed everything save our modes of thinking, and thus we drift toward unparalleled catastrophe." But if our world, because of the invention of nuclear weapons, has already departed from the traditional state of nature, then the possibility seems to open up that our choices may not be restricted to the either-or one between nuclear-armed anarchy and world government. New and more promising alternatives may be available. I believe that they are. In particular, I believe that within the framework of deterrence itself it may be possible to abolish nuclear weapons. But to understand how this might be so we need to examine deterrence more deeply—its mechanisms, its scientific and technical foundations, and its political goals.

A simple analogy may help to clarify the full novelty of the deterred state. Let us suppose that one day my neighbor comes into my house and starts to carry off my furniture. If he and I live in the civil state, I will call the police, and some organ of government will eventually decide what is to be done. If he and I live in a state of nature, there are no police or organs of government, and it is for me alone to try to stop him—by persuasion, if possible, or, if that fails, by force. Force is my last resort, the final arbiter of my dispute with my neighbor, and what then ultimately decides our dispute is whether it is he or I who lies dead on the ground. It's worth noting, though, that there is nothing inherently violent in the fact of a dispute. My neighbor may have quietly carried off my furniture while I was out. It is as a solution to the dispute that violence—or some alternative—enters the picture. In the civil state, my dispute with my neighbor is arbitrated by government, and in the state of nature it is arbitrated by the fight between him and me (if it comes to that). But when one turns to deterrence one finds that neither of these things is happening. Deterrence arbitrates nothing. Underlying the traditional belief that my neighbor and I must resolve our dispute either by violence or by government was the unstated assumption that the dispute must *be* resolved. Deterrence, however, discovers another possibility—

that disputes can be suspended, can be kept in abeyance, without any resolution. It uses terror to prevent disputes from ever coming into being. Under deterrence, I neither call the police nor shoot my neighbor—or even lay hands on him—because he doesn't enter my house to begin with. For under deterrence I have, in anticipation of my neighbor's depredations, filled my house with explosives, wired them to go off the moment any unauthorized person crosses my threshold, and (an essential step) informed my neighbor of what I have done—hoping, of course, that he will then have the good sense to give up any plans he might have for stealing my furniture. Deterrence intervenes at a point in the action quite different from that at which either force or an organ of government intervenes. Force or an organ of government steps in after the dispute has arisen and has reached an impasse, to settle it, whereas deterrence steps in before anyone has made a move, to keep the dispute from taking place.

The mechanism of deterrence is as different from the mechanism of war as its end result is from the end result of war. Deterrence is essentially psychological in its action. It uses terror to produce a mental result—the decision not to act. In the international sphere, its aim is to make government leaders *reflect* before they engage in aggression. When its action is effective, no one lies dead on the ground (although if it fails all do). It relies for its success not on the corpse of the fallen soldier but on the prudence of the live, thinking statesman. War, by contrast, while it has its psychological elements, including an element of deterrence, is in essence physical in its action: it blasts the opponent out of the way, as though he were a thing rather than a person, and his soon to be darkened psyche is of purely secondary interest.

In making deterrence possible, nuclear weapons have thus offered a new answer to the question (which lies at the heart of the nuclear predicament) of how disputes among nations are to be handled—an answer in which the disputes, instead of being arbitrated either by government or by war (or by anything else, for that matter), are kept out of "court" altogether. Because both government and war were ways of settling disputes, the civil state and the state of nature were both states of change. The deterred state, by contrast, is a stalemate. In the sphere of international politics, all is held stationary, in a sort of global-political version of "the freeze"—a version in which it is not arms that are frozen in place but national boundaries—and change is relegated to other spheres, such as the economic, the cultural, and the spiritual, and to domestic turmoil, including revolution. (Revolutionary war escapes incapacitation by nuclear weapons because the enemies—often belonging to the same families—are too closely intertwined to be able to kill one another by such indiscriminate means. Furthermore, while people have shown themselves willing to consider precipitating the annihilation of their own countries by antagonizing another nuclear power, they have yet to show themselves willing to threaten their own countries with nuclear weapons.)

Whatever may be the advantages or disadvantages of the state of deterrence, its foundations are solid. They are deeply lodged in the nature of things. They lie, in the last analysis, in the structure of matter, which we are powerless to return to its former, Newtonian state—a feat that would require us to forget twentieth-century physics. We are used to thing of deterrence as a policy, but before it is a policy it is a simple fact of life for nuclear-armed nations. Hand two nations the wherewithal to dip their buckets into the bottomless pools of energy that lie in the heart of matter and a state of deterrence springs up between them, whatever their policies may be. For their leaders, if they are rational, will grasp without the help of theory that if they drop nuclear bombs on their nuclear-armed foe, the foe may drop nuclear bombs on them in return. In the last analysis, victory is ruled out in the nuclear world because the adversaries are matched not against reserves of power that belong in any basic way to either of them individually but against the unlimited, universal power of nuclear energy, which is now more or less available to all. And what human power can hope to defeat the universe? The role of deterrence *policy* is to acknowledge, codify, and shore up this situation, and then seek certain advantages from it.

It would be a mistake, however, to suggest that the deterred state has been added to the two traditional ones, as though we were now free to choose among three states. Rather, the foundations of the traditional state of nature have themselves been altered, so that now we must distinguish between two states of nature—the prenuclear one and the nuclear one. The idea of an alteration in nature comes as something of a shock to us, as the very word ''nature'' suggest that it might. The word suggest the *given*—all that exists, has always existed, and always will exist, independent of human power to alter it. It was not in this realm that we expected alteration. We looked for alteration, on the whole, in the state, where our efforts and our will were supposed to make a difference. Whatever else might change, "anarchy" appeared to be a constant—stable, if you will. But we failed to reckon with modern physics (one of the "natural" sciences), which proved capable of transforming nature. Anarchy rested on a shaky base. When the atom was cracked open and its vast energy was spilled into our human world, anarchy's underpinnings were washed away. Thanks to physics, the supposedly changeless physical world was unexpectedly changed, and nations were simply obliged to adjust as best they could. (One of the ironies of our situation is that the natural world has proved to be more changeable than the supposedly flexible political world.)

Of course, the phrase "altering nature" is not literally accurate. In literal fact, nature remains just as it was before we pried into its secrets (as far as we know, neither the detonation of a few tens of thousands of nuclear weapons on our planet nor our disappearance as a species would have the slightest effect on any of the hundred billion or so galaxies in the universe), and what we really mean by the expression is that the physical world in which human beings live and conduct their affairs has been altered. We are not the inventors but only the discoverers of the energy in matter. The universe has always been built this way, and human beings, belonging to a rational and inquiring species, were bound to discover the fact. And then we were bound to try to figure out—as we are now doing—how to survive in such a universe. Nothing now seems more "unnatural" to us than the nuclear peril, and yet in reality nothing is more "natural," inasmuch as the peril is rooted in the basic structure of nature itself.

Whether or not one subscribes to the policy of nuclear deterrence—the threat to strike back with nuclear weapons if one's country is attacked with them or if it starts to lose a conventional war—one has to recognize as an objective fact that the equations of war and peace have had to be rewritten in our nuclear world, and that in those rewritten equations war comes out a suicidal proposition. Not only has war been taken away from us by physics—been "spoiled"—but we can't get it back. Some have tried. Among them are the devotees of "nuclear-war-fighting," who believe that it is possible to fight and survive, and even prevail in, a nuclear war, and who are now in the ascendancy in Washington. But their efforts inevitably founder in the boundless destruction of the more than a million Hiroshimas that are waiting to happen in the world's fifty-thousand-odd nuclear weapons. What these strategists can never explain is how anyone can "prevail" in a "war" after which no one would be left. Their "victories," or restorations of the peace "on terms favorable to the United States," are apparently of an extra-human sort—"victories" in which, after all the people have been killed, our bombs triumph over the other side's bombs. And the strategists' sometimes intricate and ingenious scenarios of nuclear-war-fighting are testimony only to the ability of the human mind, transported by pure abstract theory, to take leave of reality altogether.

In short, under deterrence the passage to a world in which the use of force is given up as the means of settling international differences *has already begun*. In a way, it has been accomplished. In the first days of the nuclear age, it seemed to some "idealists" that the task facing mankind was to abolish war, but realists replied that this was impossible—at least, in the short run—because it required the establishment of world government; instead, they proposed the policy of deterrence. However, when one looks at deterrence closely it turns out that war has not been preserved by it. Isn't this what the political scientist Bernard Brodie was getting at when he said, in 1946, in *The Absolute Weapon,* that in the nuclear world the only purpose of military preparations was to avert wars, not to win them? And isn't this what countless statesmen of our time have been telling us in saying that the purpose of their nuclear policies is only to prevent the use of nuclear and other weapons? The statement "War has been spoiled," which stands in such sharp contrast to Mandelbaum's "War is still possible," thus refers not to an idealistic aspiration but to a fait accompli. We cannot abolish war, because nuclear weapons have already done the job for us. What we can and must abolish is mutual assured destruction and the possibility of human extinction, the threat of which we now trade on to keep the peace. Our ambivalence toward this threat, which we try simultaneously to renounce and to exploit for our political ends, defines our new predicament. Just by thinking a little harder, and by looking a little bit more closely at both theory and practice in our nuclear world, we seemingly have already accomplished this "impossible" thing of abolishing war (among nuclear powers, anyway). This is not a mere phrase but a bedrock reality of our time, on which we may rely as we seek elements with which to build the edifice of our future safety. All the debates, carried over from the pre-nuclear age, about whether or not war is moral, and whether or not world government might be preferable, are no doubt extremely interesting, but they are anachronistic, for the world to which they have reference has gone out of existence.

Nuclear weapons, we see, have knocked the sword of war from our hands. Now it is up to us to decide what we will pick up in its place. The question before us shifts from how to abolish war to how to get along in a world from which war has been abolished. And we can start by seeing the first alternative that we have hit on—deterrence—in a new light: not as a continuation of international "anarchy," in which "war is still possible," but as *one* possible system for getting along in a world without war. Without quite recognizing it, we have taken the first steps toward global agreement. It is true that force, while it is no longer the final arbiter, or any sort of arbiter, still plays the central role, as it did in the pre-nuclear state of nature, for a by-product of force, terror, is what holds everybody immobile. Yet it is also true that, as in the civil state, each individual's force, in a kind of tacit agreement, is supposed never to be used. And, as in the civil state, the whole system depends on the recognition by each individual actor of common interest—survival—that must take precedence over individual interests. Since everybody knows and acknowledges that the use of force by any party may push everybody toward a common doom, all make efforts together to ensure that the "first use" never occurs—although at the same time each side, paradoxically, must constantly bristle with resolve to use force to repel any aggression, should it somehow occur. Moreover, right at the heart of deterrence there is an element of cooperation and consent—a crucial ingredient of every civil state, no matter how oppressive. This is the "psychological" element in deterrence, on which all else depends. For while it is true that sheer terror is the operative force in deterrence it is also true that the statesman on whom it operates must give his consent if it is to work. To be sure, his freedom of action is no greater than that of someone who is being told to do something at gunpoint; nevertheless, he remains a free agent in extremely important ways. His state of mind—his self-interest, his sanity, his prudence, his self-control, his clear-sightedness—is the real foundation of his country's and everyone else's survival. In short, he must *decide* that the world he lives in is not one in which aggression pays off. In all these respects, a deterred world is not a state of anarchy awaiting the imposition of a world order but, rather, already a sort of world order, albeit one that is in many ways contradictory and absurd.

In a deep sense, unless the species does destroy itself our world will remain a deterred world. By this I do not mean that we shall forever maintain nuclear weapons and threaten one another with mutual assured destruction. I mean that whether we possess nuclear weapons or abolish them the terror they inspire will dominate our affairs and dictate the character of our political decisions. Even if mankind were now to enter formally into the civil state, and found a world government to replace war, deterrence would, in a way, still be in effect. In the pre-nuclear world, entry into the civil state would have been a free act, arising out of an abundant faith in humanity and confidence in its betterment. For us, however, who live surrounded by doom, like people in a town at the foot of a rumbling volcano (it is our peculiar distinction not to have built our town next to Vesuvius but to have built Vesuvius next to our town), entry into the civil state would be a compelled act: a measure taken not so much to better life as only to hold on to it—not to bring heaven to earth but only to preserve the earth. Being inspired by terror, entry into the civil state would be a variant of the balance of terror under deterrence—a variant in which nations, instead of deterring each other from starting a nuclear holocaust, would all join together to deter the species as a whole from extinguishing itself. While the shift from multiplicity to unity would require a global political revolution—it would be some equivalent of what Einstein called for—even that revolution would not suspend the underlying transformation of human existence which was brought about by the development of nuclear weapons. We can never recover war. We will always be at risk, somewhere down the road, of extinguishing ourselves. We will always live in a state of deterrence. These changes mark a transformation of our world. And it is this transformed world, not the vanished, pre-nuclear one, that is our true starting point as we face the nuclear peril.

The great aim—the supreme good—that we seek through deterrence is "stability." However, this aim, to which we often refer as though it were single and indivisible, actually comprises two separate and conflicting aims. The first is to preserve the political stalemate—to freeze the status quo. The status quo in question is the one that was more or less fixed in place (at least in the central theatres of superpower rivalry, where the influence of nuclear weapons made itself felt most keenly) in the years immediately following the Second World War. What recommended this status quo as the one in which to freeze the world was not the virtue of its particular arrangements—in fact, terrible injustices, including Soviet domination of Eastern Europe, were institutionalized by it—but only the fact that it *was* the status quo when the nuclear age began, and was thus the logical starting place for a system whose essence was going to be that no changes through military action were permitted. In a broader sense, however, the status quo was the system of independent states, which had existed throughout history but whose continued existence was called into question by the nuclear peril. The second aim is to avert a nuclear holocaust, which the great powers hope to head off by the paradoxical, jujitsulike means of threatening one another (if only in retaliation) with that same holocaust. In other words, the policy seeks to give satisfactory resolutions of the two great issues that were raised by the development of nuclear weapons—*how* man should live (in nation-states or in some other way; under capitalism, Communism, or something else; and so on) and *whether* he would live.

The principle that binds these two aims of deterrent policy together, and whose observance would make them obtainable simultaneously, is the principle of nonaggression. This principle embodies no millennial dreams, yet its realization has been much sought (through the League of Nations and the United Nations, among other organizations) and rarely achieved. Nuclear weapons lend tremendous support to the principle of nonaggression. Traditionally, victory—the light at the end of the tunnel of war—has been the great incentive for aggression; but nuclear weapons have killed this hope in the breasts of all realistic government leaders and have thus robbed aggression of its point. Confusingly—and regrettably—they have robbed defense of *its* point, too, since in a nuclear "war" the defender is as thoroughly annihilated as the aggressor. For both parties, the tunnel of war now leads only to eternal darkness. The development of nuclear weapons has therefore, at least in theory, laid the foundation for a world at peace. And, in fact, ever since the balance of terror was established the great powers have enjoyed the stability promised by deterrence. They have never used military force against one another, although the air has been filled with threats (which are of the essence of deterrence), and although they have felt free to use their forces against non-nuclear powers. No one has liked this stalemate very much, yet people have made do with it. It is "acceptable": we have accepted it.

No one knows what any of the statesmen of our day would really do if, in the moment of truth, they were forced to choose between the two goals of deterrence policy, and either suffer military defeat or launch a nuclear holocaust. But there can be no doubt about which course the doctrine of deterrence specifies: it specifies the holocaust. If it doesn't specify the holocaust, then it isn't deterrence but something else. In that sense, deterrence gives a clear priority to national defense over human survival (although government leaders, of course, hope never to have to make the choice). If this weren't so, the resolution of the nuclear predicament would be easy. We could simply "ban the bomb," and let political matters sort themselves out however they might. If human survival had been the world's overriding goal from the time the nuclear threat first presented itself, and *not* to use nuclear weapons had really been the dominant consideration in nuclear policy—that is, if people had been ready to risk or sacrifice their particular ways of life for the sake of life itself (not their individual lives but the survival of the species)—then they would have at least seriously considered either disarming unilaterally or establishing world government, or doing both. Sometimes it is suggested that unilateral disarmament might itself lead to the use of nuclear weapons, because by creating a military imbalance it would invite the very aggression that the disarmers were hoping to head off. This argument, however, holds true only for half-hearted, faltering unilateral disarmament, which would be reversed as soon as an enemy attack materialized. Thoroughgoing, resolute disarmament would not lead to any use of nuclear arms, because the enemy could get what it wanted from the now militarily undefended country simply by walking into it. What unilateral disarmament might really lead to is not a nuclear holocaust but military defeat and foreign occupation. If by "stability" we meant only the absence of war, then unilateral disarmament would be a matchless way of achieving it. Defeat could be entirely "stable."

In the present context, however, the point is not to advocate or oppose either unilateral disarmament or world government but only to make it clear that the rejection of both by just about everybody in favor of a policy of deterrence shows that the principal goal of deterrence is to preserve national sovereignty and everything that goes with sovereignty. At the very heart of the riddle of deterrence sits sovereignty, whose preservation the policy achieves by subjecting mankind to the risk of extinction. Whatever final judgment one might make on this bargain—and it is extreme dissatisfaction with it that has fuelled the new peace movement—the arguments in its favor are substantial enough not to require obfuscation by the misleading claim that we possess nuclear arms chiefly in order to avoid using them. National sovereignty *in itself*—the full political control by local people of their own territories—is, most people would agree, highly desirable. Certainly most people treasure the independence of their own countries. And probably very few even of those whose countries are not defended by nuclear arsenals would like to see either the establishment of a world government or the collapse of the balance of terror through unilateral disarmament. Furthermore, liberty in the world at large may depend on the political survival of a certain number of countries, including, above all, the democracies of the West. The strongest and most honest argument in favor of the possession of nuclear weapons, then—for those who believe in liberty—is that upholding liberty is worth the risk of extinction. (For the Soviet government, of course, the justification would be that socialism is upheld.) The argument is strengthened if one maintains—as the Catholic bishops, in their pastoral letter, and Brodie do, but *Living with Nuclear Weapons* does not—that deterrence is a temporary, emergency arrangement, soon to be replaced by some better system, in which we no longer secure our safety by threatening our doom.

Nevertheless, it remains true that, within the limits imposed by the fundamental decision to defend national sovereignty with nuclear arsenals, the mutual-assured-destruction strategists do, as an additional goal, seek to deploy the weapons in such a way as to reduce to a minimum the chance of a holocaust. They do their best to see to it that the threat of annihilation by which sovereignty is preserved also prevents the execution of the threat. Above all, they seek to adopt strategic policies that add to stability—by, for example, building retaliatory rather than first-strike weapons, forgoing attempts at civil defense, establishing hot lines and the like with the adversary, and, of course, entering into arms-control agreements. (It is regarding these measures, which assume the existence of nuclear arsenals, that the sometimes arcane disputes between the advocates of mutual assured destruction and the advocates of nuclear-war-fighting take place, with the mutual-assured-destruction school, on the whole, favoring measures that will stop the holocaust from ever occurring in the first place and the nuclear-war-fighting school favoring measures that would supposedly enable the United States to get some advantage over the Soviet Union if a holocaust did occur.)

Such are the means and ends of the doctrine of deterrence, on which we rely today for the safety of the nuclear world. They present us with a striking disparity. The over-all end—the military stalemate—is modest and conservative. The means, however—two nations' threats to annihilate one another and, perhaps, all mankind—are extreme in a way that gives new meaning to that word. The problem with deterrence is not that it doesn't "work"—it is, I am sure, a very effective (though far from infallible) way of restraining the superpowers from attacking one another, should they be inclined to do so—but that we must pay an inconceivable price if it fails. Regarded as a sort of world order, deterrence is a regime in which every crime is punished by the severest possible penalty, as though the ruler of a state had decreed that if just one of the citizens commits a a burglary all the citizens must be put to death. This radical disproportion between ends and means invites us to inquire whether we might not be able to achieve our modest ends by less extreme means—a means by which we did not threaten ourselves with doom. This definition of our task is, of course, quite different from the one in which we were invited to found world government in the midst of "anarchy" or else accept a life lived perpetually on the edge of extinction. Now we would be working within deterrence defined in its broadest sense—as the new "state of nature," brought into being by the very peril that we wish to alleviate. This could come about because deterrence offers us elements to work with that were not available in the pre-nuclear age. Two stand out. The first is the stalemate itself, which was made possible only because of the fearsome destructive power of the military invention that backs it up. The second is the unlosable nature of the knowledge that underlies the invention, and prevents us from ever wholly expunging the possibility of nuclear destruction from our affairs.

Our first step would be to accept the political verdict that has been delivered by deterrence, and formalize the stalemate. The achievement of the stalement was, in the broadest sense, accidental: conceived as a makeshift for coping in the short term with a sudden peril that the world lacked either the imagination or the will (or both) to tackle head-on, it gradually took shape, over a period of decades, through trial and error. Its creation was the principal work of a generation. The question for that generation (once world government and full nuclear disarmament were jointly ruled out) was whether, given the presence of nuclear weapons in the world, stability could be achieved. It could be. It was. But now, with the answer to that question in hand, we can start with stability—the stalemate—and invert the question, asking whether, within the new context of our transformed world, there might not be a better means of preserving that same stability: a means with less extreme risk attached. What for the people of the earlier generation was the end point of their efforts can for us be the starting point. For even as we see that deterrence is possible we know, and have felt in our hearts, that the bargain now struck by it is unworthy of human life, because it turns us into potential mass slayers of our species. The lesson, too, is a fruit of our experience in the nuclear age, and it drives us to seek to dismantle the doomsday machine at the earliest possible moment. A deepening awareness of the full meaning of that bargain—frequently and rightly described as "Faustian"—for strategy, for the state of our civilization, and for the state of our souls is what now inspires the world's gathering protest against nuclear arms.

Our method can be to convert into a settlement in principle the settlement of political differences which we have achieved in fact under the pressure of the nuclear threat. We can, in a manner of speaking, adopt our present world, with all its injustices and other imperfections, as our ideal, and then seek the most sensible and moderate means of preserving it. This effort is consistent with the spiritual task that nuclear weapons have put before us, which is at bottom to awaken ourselves to a new appreciation and gratitude for the world that is given to each of us at birth. For the time being, instead of asking ourselves how, in the light of the peril to all life, we must transform all life, we ask what the best way is to keep everything just the same. Not improvement but mere continuation is our dream. This, of course, is a deeply conservative aim, but then the nuclear peril seems to call on us to be conservative, inasmuch as *conserving* ourselves and our world is the challenge that we now face. To many peoples, the idea of freezing the status quo might seem discouraging, especially if for them the status quo includes intervention in their affairs by a great power. The peoples of Eastern Europe are a case in point. They cannot wish to formalize Soviet domination of their countries. The formalization of the status quo envisioned here, however, would not do that. It would permit those peoples every means to liberate themselves that they now have at their disposal, and would remove only means that they now already lack—Western military intervention in their struggles.

The next question is whether, after formalizing the status quo, we can reduce our reliance on the extreme means by which we now uphold it, and how far a reduction can go. The invaluable lesson of deterrence theory is that in the nuclear age the use of force is self-cancelling. This is the profound truth that the statesmen of our day are struggling to articulate when—expressing, no doubt, their fervent desire, though it is not the actual case—they tell us that they possess nuclear weapons only in order *not* to use them. At first, the simple and almost irresistible implication of that truth for policy seems to be that we can take the whole hateful machinery of force—conventional and nuclear—and clear it out of our lives. The moment we did that, all the paradoxes, contradictions, absurdities, and abominations that we live with under deterrence would evaporate. If the whole doomsday machine is intended only to paralyze itself—to do nothing—why do we need it? Can't we accomplish nothing without threatening suicide? But the very question reveals that after all—semi-covertly and somewhat shamefacedly—we actually rely on the doomsday machine to serve another end: the preservation of our sovereignty. We still exploit the peril of extinction for our political ends. And we don't know how to wean ourselves from that reliance without taking radical steps, such as unilateral disarmament or world government. But while some of us may be ready for radical steps the world as a whole, it is clear, is not, and demands that we preserve the sovereignty of states, even though it requires a risk to our survival. Given this political reality—which shows no sign of changing soon—it appears that, in one form or another, our reliance on the nuclear threat cannot be broken. Nevertheless, even under these terms we have far more flexibility than we have thought. It is a flexibility that, I believe, extends all the way to the abolition of nuclear arms.

On the face of it, there appears to be a contradiction between the two goals we have set for ourselves. It appears that we want to keep the stalemate but to abolish the weapons that make it possible. Yet this contradiction exists in present policy—taking the form of our threatening to use the weapons in order *not* to use them. Either way, paradox is our lot. We seek to preserve a stalemated, purely defensive world but must apparently

make use of—or at least make provision for—purely offensive weapons to do it. Indeed, one way of looking at
the nuclear predicament is to see it as the final outcome
of a competition between offense and defense which has
been going on throughout the history of war, in a sort
of war within war. The invention of nuclear weapons
gave the victory once and for all, it appears, to the offensive side. Although the unpredictability of science
prevents a truly definitive judgment, the chances that
the defense will ever catch up look vanishingly dim.
The entire history of warfare supports this conclusion:
although the balance between offense and defense has
swung back and forth, the general trend has been un-
varyingly toward the increasing destructiveness of offensive war. It is this rising general destructiveness, and
not the recent success of one particular offensive
weapon in eluding destruction by a defensive counter-
part, that has now culminated in the whole planet's
being placed in mortal peril. The ultimate vulnerability
of human beings is the result of the frailty of nature itself, on which we depend utterly for life; as is now
clearer to us than ever before, nature cannot stand up to
much nuclear destruction. Given this flood tide of destructive power, which was rising steadily even before
nuclear weapons were developed, and has continued
since their development (in the fields of chemical and
biological warfare, for example), the hopes for defense
are not so much slight as beside the point. Most of these
hopes rest on weapons that counter not the effects of nuclear weapons but, rather, the nuclear weapons' delivery vehicles. Yet a delivery vehicle is simply anything
that gets from point A to point B on the face of the earth.
A horse and cart is a delivery vehicle. An army battling

its way into enemy territory is a delivery vehicle. A man with a suitcase is a delivery vehicle. There seems little chance that all existing vehicles—not to mention all the vehicles that science will dream up in the future—can be decisively countered. And it is even more unlikely that the devices designed to attack all the delivery vehicles would remain invulnerable to devices that scientists would soon be inventing to attack *them*. The superiority of the offense in a world of uninhibited production of nuclear weapons and their delivery vehicles therefore appears to be something that will last for the indefinite future.

The contradiction between the end we seek and the means of attaining it becomes even clearer when we try to imagine the situation we would have if in 1945 the scientists, instead of handing us the ultimate offensive weapon, had emerged from their laboratory with an ultimate defensive weapon—perhaps one of those impenetrable bubbles with which science-fiction writers like to surround cities. Then a thoroughgoing, consistent defensive world would be possible. Aggressively inclined nations might hurl their most lethal weapons at their neighbors, but the weapons would all bounce off harmlessly, and no one would be hurt. Peoples would then live safely within their own borders, suffering only the torments that they managed to invent for themselves. Under our present circumstances, by contrast, we have not perfect defense but perfect vulnerability.

It was in addressing this contradiction that the strategists came up with the doctrine of deterrence in the first place. Their chief discovery was that the threat of retaliation could substitute for the missing defenses. But while defense and deterrence have the same ends the way they work is nearly opposite. In a defensive system, you rely on your military forces actually to throw the enemy forces back: the swung sword falls on the raised shield without inflicting damage; the advancing foot soldier falls into the moat; the warhead is pulverized by the laser beam. But in a system of deterrence you have given up all hope of throwing the enemy back, and are hoping instead, by threatening a retaliatory attack that *he* cannot throw back, to dissuade him from attacking at all. Deterrence thus rests on the fear of a double offense, in which everyone would destroy everyone else and no one would be defended. The crucial element in deterrence is the foreknowledge by the potential aggressor that if he starts anything this is how it will end. Offensive means are made to serve defensive ends. But in the process the continuation of our species is put in jeopardy.

Inasmuch as the goal we have chosen is to shore up a stalemated, defensive world, one way of defining our task would be to ask whether, having agreed to live with the status quo, we might by further agreement accomplish what we are unable to accomplish through technical efforts; namely, to snatch the victory away from offensive arms and hand it, at least provisionally, back to defensive ones. The question is whether as political and diplomatic actors we could rush into the fray on the side of the defense and turn the tables. I think that, within certain all-important limits, we can. The key is to enter into an agreement abolishing nuclear arms. Nations would first agree, in effect, to drop their swords from their hands and lift their shields toward one another instead. They would agree to have not world government, in which all nations are fused into one nation, but its exact opposite—a multiplicity of inviolate nations pledged to leave each other alone. For nations that now possess nuclear weapons, the agreement would be a true abolition agreement. For those that do not now possess them, it would be a strengthened nonproliferation agreement. (A hundred and nineteen nations have already signed the nonproliferation treaty of 1968.) Obviously, an agreement among the superpowers on both the nature of the status quo and the precise terms of abolition would be the most difficult part of the negotiation. The agreement would be enforced not by any world police force or other organ of a global state but by each nation's knowledge that a breakdown of the agreement would be to no one's advantage, and would only push all nations back down the path to doom. In the widest sense, the agreement would represent the institutionalization of this knowledge. But if nuclear weapons are to be abolished by agreement, one might ask, why not go all the way? Why not abolish conventional weapons and defensive weapons as well? The answer, of course, is that even in the face of the threat of annihilation nations have as yet shown no willingness to surrender their sovereignty, and conventional arms would be one support for its preservation. While the abolition of nuclear arms would increase the margin of mankind's safety against nuclear destruction and the peril of extinction, the retention of conventional arms would permit the world to hold on to the system of nation-states. Therefore, a second provision of the agreement would stipulate that the size of conventional forces be limited and balanced. In keeping with the defensive aim of the agreement as a whole, these forces would, to whatever extent this was technically possible, be deployed and armed in a defensive mode.

There is also another reason for retaining defenses. One of the most commonly cited and most substantial reasons for rejecting the abolition of nuclear arms, even if the nuclear powers should develop the will to abolish them, is that the verification of a nuclear-abolition agreement could never be adequate. And, as far as I know, it is true that no one has ever devised a system of verification that could, even theoretically, preclude significant cheating. Like defense, it seems, inspection is almost inherently imperfect. When arsenals are large, the argument runs, a certain amount of cheating on arms-control agreements is unimportant, because the number of concealed weapons is likely to be small in relation to the size of the arsenals as a whole. But as the size of the arsenals shrinks, it is said, the importance of cheating grows, and finally the point is reached at which the hidden arsenals tip the strategic balance in favor of the cheater. According to this argument, the point of maximum—indeed, total—imbalance is reached when, after an abolition agreement has been signed, one side cheats while the other does not. Then the cheater, it is said, has an insuperable advantage, and holds its innocent and trusting cosigner at its mercy. But if antinuclear defenses are retained the advantage in cheating is sharply reduced, or actually eliminated. Arrayed against today's gigantic nuclear forces, defenses are helpless. Worse, one side's defenses serve as a goad to further offensive production by the other side, which doesn't want the offensive capacity it has decided on to be weakened. But if defenses were arrayed against the kind of force that could be put together in violation of an abolition agreement they could be crucial. On the one side would be a sharply restricted, untested, and clandestinely produced and maintained offensive force, while on the other side would be a large, fully tested, openly deployed, and technically advanced defensive force. Such a force might not completely nullify the danger of cheating (there is always the man with a suitcase), but no one can doubt that it would drastically reduce it. At the very least, it would throw the plans of an aggressor into a condition of total uncertainty. Moreover, as the years passed after the signing of the agreement the superiority of the defense would be likely to increase, because defensive weapons would continue to be openly developed, tested, and deployed, while offensive weapons could not be. Therefore—probably as a separate, third provision of the agreement—anti-nuclear defensive forces would be permitted.

President Reagan recently offered a vision of a world protected from nuclear destruction by defensive weapons, many of which would be based in space. The United States, he said, should develop these weapons and then share them with the Soviet Union. With both countries protected from nuclear attack, he went on, both would be able to scrap their now useless nuclear arsenals and achieve full nuclear disarmament. Only the order of events in his proposal was wrong. If we seek first to defend ourselves, and not to abolish nuclear weapons until after we have made that effort, we will never abolish them, because of the underlying, technically irreversible superiority of the offensive in the nuclear world. But if we abolish nuclear weapons first and then build the defenses, as a hedge against cheating, we can succeed. Abolition prepares the way for defense.

However, none of these defensive arrangements would offer much protection if the agreement failed to accompany them with one more provision. The worst case—which must be taken into account if nations are to have confidence in the military preparations for thwarting aggressors—is not mere cheating but blatant, open violation of the agreement by a powerful and ruthless nation that is determined to intimidate or subjugate other nations, or the whole world, by suddenly and swiftly building up, and perhaps actually using, an overwhelming nuclear arsenal. This possibility creates the all-important limits mentioned earlier. As soon as it happened, the underlying military superiority of the offensive in the nuclear world would again hold sway, and the conventional and anti-nuclear defenses permitted under the abolition agreement would become useless. (Just how soon in this buildup the offensive weapons would eclipse the defensive ones would depend on the effectiveness of the defenses that had been built up.) The only significant military response to this threat would be a response in kind: a similar nuclear buildup by the threatened nations, returning the world to something like the balance of terror as we know it today. But in order to achieve that buildup the threatened nations would probably have to have already in existence considerable preparations for the manufacture of nuclear arms. Therefore, a fourth provision of the abolition agreement would permit nations to hold themselves in a particular, defined state of readiness for nuclear rearmament. This provision would, in fact, be the very core of the military side of the agreement. It would be the definition, in technical terms, of what "abolition" was to be. And it would be the final guarantor of the safety of nations against attack. However, this guarantor would not defend. It would deter. The most important element in this readiness would simply be the knowledge of how to make the weapons—knowledge that nations are powerless to get rid of even if they want to. This unlosable knowledge is, as we have seen, the root fact of life in the nuclear world, from which the entire predicament proceeds. But, just as the potential for nuclear aggression flows from the knowledge, menacing the stability of the agreement, so does the potential for retaliation, restoring the stability of the agreement. Its persistence is the reason that deterrence doesn't dissolve when the weapons are abolished. In other words, in the nuclear world the threat to use force is as self-cancelling at zero nuclear weapons as it is at fifty thousand nuclear weapons. Thus, both in its political ends—preservation of a stalemate—and in its means—using the threat of nuclear destruction itself to prevent the use of nuclear weapons—the abolition agreement would represent an extension of the doctrine of deterrence: an extension in which the most terrifying features of the doctrine would be greatly mitigated, although not finally removed.

The agreed-upon preparations would be based on the knowledge. In all likelihood, they would consist both of inspectable controls on nuclear reactors and on other facilities producing weapons-grade materials and of rules regarding the construction of delivery vehicles. One question that the policymakers would put to the scientists would be what precise level of technical arrangements would permit some particular, defined level of armament to be achieved in a fixed lead time to nuclear rearmament—say, six weeks. Possible lead times would be defined in such terms as the following: an eight-week lead time to the production of two hundred warheads mounted on cruise missiles, or a six-week lead time to a hundred warheads mounted in military aircraft. The lead time would have to be short enough so that the would-be aggressor, seeking to make use of the interval as a head start, would not be able to establish a decisive lead. ''Decisive'' in this, or any, nuclear context refers to the ability to destroy the victim's retaliatory capacity in a preemptive first strike. Preemption is the spectre that haunts the deterrence strategists, for if one side can destroy the retaliatory capacity of the other side in a preemptive strike, then deterrence dissolves. This is the point at which victory looms up again as a possibility, and force stops being self-cancelling. (At least, it does in the short run. It's much more difficult to see how a nuclear aggressor could escape retaliation over a longer run.) So it is today, and so it would be in a world of zero nuclear weapons.

The task for strategy in a nuclear-weapon-free world would be to design a capacity for nuclear rearmament which could not be destroyed in a first strike by a nation that took the lead in rearmament by abrogating the abolition agreement, secretly or openly. Retaliatory capacity would have to be able to keep pace with aggressive capacity—to the extent that a disarming first strike would be excluded. If that requirement was satisfied, possession in a nuclear-weapon-free world of the capacity for rebuilding nuclear weapons would deter nations from rebuilding them and then using them, just as in our present, nuclear-armed world possession of the weapons themselves deters nations from using them. Today, missile deters missile, bomber deters bomber, submarine deters submarine. Under what we might call weaponless deterrence, factory would deter factory, blueprint would deter blueprint, equation would deter equation. In today's world, when the strategists assess one another's arsenals they see that every possible escalation in attack can be matched by an escalation on the other side, until the arsenals of both sides are depleted and both nations are annihilated. So the two sides are deterred from attacking one another. With weaponless deterrence in effect, the strategists would see that any possible escalation in rearmament by one side could be matched by an escalation on the other side, until both were again fully armed and ready to embark on mutual assured destruction. So they would be deterred from rearming.

It has often been said that the impossibility of uninventing nuclear weapons makes their abolition impossible. But under the agreement described here the opposite would be the case. The knowledge of how to rebuild the weapons is just the thing that would make abolition *possible,* because it would keep deterrence in force. Indeed, the everlastingness of the knowledge is the key to the abolition of nuclear arms within the framework of deterrence. Once we accept the fact that the acquisition of the knowledge was the essential preparation for nuclear armament, and that it can never be reversed, we can see that every state of disarmament is also a state of armament. And, being a state of armament, it has deterrent value. In pointing out the deterrent value of preparations for nuclear rearmament, and even of the mere knowledge of how to rebuild the weapons, we make the reply to the present opponents of abolition which Bernard Brodie made to Robert Oppenheimer. Oppenheimer, rightly observing that nuclear weapons could not be defended against, called them inherently ''aggressive'' weapons and predicted that they would inevitably be used in lightning-swift aggressive war. In such a world, of course, there would have been no stability whatever. But to this Brodie responded that the would-be aggressor would not be the only one possessing nuclear weapons, and that when the aggressor saw that its foe possessed them—and was ready to retaliate with them—its aggressive fever would be cooled down. Now we are told that aggressors will take advantage of the abolition of nuclear weapons to rebuild and use nuclear weapons, and to this the answer again is that the intended victims will have the same capacities, and these will act as a deterrent, saving the world's stability.

The notion that abolition is impossible because uninvention is impossible appears to stem from a failure to distinguish clearly between these two things. The confusion is exemplified in *Living with Nuclear Weapons*, in which, in support of their conclusion that a world without nuclear weapons is ''a fictional utopia,'' the Harvard authors write, ''The discovery of nuclear weapons, like the discovery of fire itself, lies behind us on the trajectory of history: it cannot be undone. Even if all nuclear arsenals were destroyed, the knowledge of how to reinvent them would remain and could be put to use in any of a dozen or more nations. The atomic fire cannot be extinguished.'' The authors fear that ''the knowledge of how to reinvent'' the weapons will upset any abolition agreement. But if one has ''the knowledge,'' there is no need to ''reinvent'' anything, because one can go ahead and rebuild the weapons right away by using that knowledge. If, on the other hand, reinvention is really required, then one must have somehow lost the knowledge, but this is impossible. Of course, if one speaks of the knowledge of how to rebuild the weapons rather than "the knowledge of how to reinvent" them, the inconsistency disappears; but then one is speaking of rearming after abolition rather than after uninvention. By inadvertently blurring the distinction between the two, the Harvard authors, like many other proponents of deterrence, make abolition appear to be, like uninvention, impossible, and confer upon the world's nuclear arsenals a durability and irremovability that in fact only the knowledge of how to make them possesses. Though uninvention is impossible, abolition is not. Or if it were true that both were impossible it would have to be for completely different reasons—in the case of uninvention because we don't know how to rid the world of basic scientific knowledge, and in the case of abolition because we lack the necessary political will. If the distinction is kept clear, then the hope opens up that the impossibility of uninvention, which is the fundamental fact of life in the nuclear world, makes abolition, which is just one of the conceivable ways of organizing that world, possible. For it was the invention, not the buildup, of nuclear arms that irreversibly placed mankind within reach of its own self-slaughtering hand, ruined war as the final arbiter in global affairs, and set mankind adrift in a new and unfamiliar political world.

The stages of nuclear escalation are often pictured as a ladder reaching from a peaceful but nuclear-armed world up through various levels of nuclear attack and retaliation to the end of the world. Deterrence calls for the ability of each potential adversary to match the others at each rung of the ladder. The levels of nuclear armament, from zero up to a full-scale doomsday machine, can be pictured as lower rungs on that same ladder, and the levels of technical and industrial preparation for the production of nuclear arms as still lower rungs. On this extended ladder, the bottom rung is not zero nuclear weapons but the bare knowledge of how to make them, unaccompanied by any preparations to rebuild them. In actuality, however, this lowest rung can never be reached, because every general level of technical proficiency, whether geared to weapons production or not, is a state of readiness for nuclear armament at one level or another. That is why there can be no such thing as a return to the pre-nuclear world but only increases in the lead time to nuclear armament and from there to a holocaust. At present, the lead time is virtually the shortest possible: we might say that it is seven minutes—approximately the time that it would take for forward-based strategic missiles on each side to reach targets in the opposing country. If world government, or some equivalent political solution, were in place, the lead time might arguably be centuries, but there would still *be* a lead time, because the knowledge of how to build nuclear weapons would remain in the world. Under the abolition agreement described here, our modest but invaluable achievement would be in increasing this lead time from its present seven minutes to weeks or months.

The technical choice available to us, then, is not whether to possess or to eradicate nuclear weapons but what should be the state of readiness—or, if you want to look at it that way, of unreadiness—for nuclear hostilities in which, by international agreement, we would hold the world. The either-or character of the choice between deterrence with full-scale nuclear arsenals and world government without them no longer has to paralyze the world, for we find that within deterrence itself there are endless gradations, leading all the way down to zero and beyond, as the state of readiness is reduced and diplomatic and political arrangements are improved. Deterrence has more extensive possibilities than we have yet acknowledged. It is our curse—a kind of second fall from grace—that the knowledge of how to extinguish ourselves as a species will never leave us. And it is perhaps only modest compensation that that same knowledge, by ruining war—a lesser but more ancient curse under which our species has labored—has laid the foundations for a world at peace. Nevertheless, to throw this advantage away would be a monumental mistake, since it is one of the few elements that work in our favor as we seek to avoid extinction. The durability of the invention and the collapse of war which has come with it provide a strong foundation on which to begin to build our safety. But on this strong foundation we have so far built only a rickety, improvised shelter. We suffer the danger that flows from the fact that the fateful knowledge is inexpungible from our world, but we have so far turned down the advantages that flow from that fact. We arrange to terrorize one another with annihilation, but we have so far failed to achieve the full measure of safety obtainable from the terror. It is a paradox fully worthy of this elaborate doctrine that if we were to permit ourselves to recognize clearly the breadth and depth of the peril—to assure ourselves once and for all of its boundlessness and durability—we might thereby clear a path to our salvation.

Deterrence depends on foreknowledge. Without that, we have no barrier between ourselves and our doom. It is a system in which government leaders who might be inclined toward aggression look at the end of the story they would be setting in motion, see their own and everyone else's doom written there, and therefore decide not to take even the first step. Deterrence under an abolition agreement would work in precisely the same way, except that the story at the end of which doom was written would be somewhat longer and the foreknowledge a little farther-sighted. It would now take in all the rungs on the ladder, from the construction of the first nuclear weapon up to the end of the world. The changeover from today's system would be less drastic than it might at first appear. Even under the present doctrine, the weapons are only "psychological" arsenals, meant to create terrifying "appearances." Their targets are not people's bodies; but their minds, and, theoretically, the weapons' physical destiny is to rust into powder in their silos, or to pass into honored retirement, as a new and still more fearsome "generation" is groomed to take their place. Indeed, because they are wholly devoted to creating the right menacing appearances and inducing the right states of mind, no one has ever been able to suggest any sensible or sane mission for them "if deterrence fails" and the moment for their supposed actual use arrives. The manifest failure of the nuclear-war-fighters to fill the gap only underscores the point. Furthermore, the weapons have been pulled back to a purely responsive—if not exactly a "defensive"—role.

Everyone says that he will use them only if he is attacked. So, theoretically, if everyone behaves well, and no one attacks, no one will use them. (Unfortunately, though, if someone does attack we are committed to using them.) In military history (if we can call such unalloyed posturing ''military''), these arsenals are unique in that they can fail simply by being employed in action. They have become semi-real, shadow things, designed to play a merely supporting role in a public-relations game. This role could be filled just as well by a sham, papier-mâché arsenal, if only we could be sure that the fraud would not be discovered. Abolition would carry the present quasi-retirement of the weapons one more step. Instead of literal-mindedly requiring that we keep the actual physical things under our noses to frighten ourselves with, we would make do with the capacity for rebuilding them, which should be frightening enough.

In chess, when skilled players reach a certain point in the play they are able to see that, no matter what further moves are made, the outcome is determined, and they end the game without going through the motions. This is also our situation in the nuclear world—with the difference that the predetermined outcome is not the victory of one side or the other but the destruction of both. The difference between our present world and a nuclear-weapon-free world would be only that people had all learned to see a few steps farther ahead than they do now—as though the chess players, having gained in experience, were to call off their game four moves before checkmate rather than two. Every statesman would see, just as he does today, that aggression leads inevitably to annihilation, and would feel no need to test the proposition in action. This does not seem too much for people to have learned after thirty-nine years of staring oblivion in the face.

The great advantage of our present situation is that by actually having built a doomsday machine we have played all the moves in this game except the last, and so know from experience, as people in the first years of the nuclear age could not, where the moves lead. We've played the game this far, and the result of the final moves is before our eyes—not the victory of one side over the other but doom. If mankind were ever to lift the nuclear peril, one saying that people might employ to keep themselves from backsliding would be "Remember 1984." (But if we use 1984 to turn the nuclear-arms race around we might give this year, prospectively slated for infamy by George Orwell, a place of honor.) It seems likely that, to an extent that we today can hardly begin to imagine, future generations, if there are any, will look back on our recent history with unutterable horror. They will recall incredulously a generation that, bowing down abjectly to a technical device of its own invention, set up the machinery for the destruction of humanity. They are likely to look back with particular incredulity, it seems to me, on us in the West. The world must count on us in the West to take the lead in resolving the nuclear predicament, because we enjoy freedom here, including the freedom to examine the nuclear predicament in a creative and unfettered way. But of what avail will our freedom have been to us and to the world if by making use of it we arrive only at fatalism? Perhaps it will be concluded in defense of our generation as a whole that it was *necessary* to build the doomsday machine, so that, like a child that makes a mask to frighten itself with, we could make the nuclear peril real to ourselves—real enough so that we would finally do something about it. If that is so, we could regard the nuclear-arms race of the last several decades as a gigantic educational device—a sort of classroom aid designed to teach us all about nuclear weapons and the doom they portend. (Such a role would be consistent with the ''psychological'' role which we now assign to the weapons in strategic doctrine.) The result offered by this perilous exercise, at any rate, is the advantage that we have over people who faced the question in 1945. But if we fail to avail ourselves of the advantage—if we fail to learn the lesson that our indirect experience offers—then there will be little to be said in our favor, and perhaps no one to say it.

Before we examine in greater detail how an abolition agreement might work, a cautionary word seems in order concerning hypothetical constructions of future events—or ''scenarios,'' as they are called—and, in particular, scenarios involving deterrence. We want to arrive at a judgment about the general workability of an abolition agreement under which an ability to rebuild nuclear weapons would serve as a deterrent. The key word is ''judgment.'' It is emphatically not ''prediction.'' Judgment never claims certainty; it never pretends to *know* what the future holds. It is not a science, and in a world dominated by the relative certainties of science and the pseudocertainties of pseudoscience its admittedly fallible claims often fail to command respect. Judgment does not rely on reason alone; it also summons into play intuition, emotion, experience, temperament—in a sense, our whole being. But in the nuclear field judgment has a competitor—strategic "theory," which tries, like science, to proceed by reasoning. Strategic theory, however, lacks an element that is crucial to science: empirical verification. There is always the danger with theory that it will come to supplant reality in the minds of the theorists; and in nuclear-strategic theorizing the danger is especially acute, because, fortunately, mankind has had no direct experience of "nuclear war"—of two-sided nuclear combat—against which to measure its hypotheses. Strategic theory is in that respect like a physics without the benefit of experimentation, or a social science without the benefit of a society to observe. Never, perhaps, has pure deduction, uncorrected by empirical knowledge, been given freer rein or assigned a more important role in the regulation of human affairs.

When experience is replaced by theory, the possibility always exists that the theory's assumptions will be generally accepted as conclusions. One particularly harmful assumption of this kind in the theory of deterrence is that only the balance of terror counts in the decision-making of statesmen, so that if your adversary gets the slightest opening to do his worst to you he will do it. The effect of making this assumption is to introduce into policy an extreme reductionism, in which moral and psychological, and even diplomatic and political, influences on governmental conduct are ruled out of consideration. And since deterrence is not merely a theory but a policy there is a further danger that this reductionist assumption can take on the quality of a self-fulfilling prophecy. Two nations, starting by assuming unmitigated enmity between them, and proceeding on both sides to build their military forces accordingly, can soon find that the unmitigated enmity has become real. It has become a fact that each side menaces the other with annihilation, and this fact has emotional and psychological consequences of its own, independent of any prior, underlying enmity. At this point, the assumption, which may at the beginning have masked a more complex and subtly shaded reality, has become "true." The British historian E. P. Thompson has pointed out, in his recent book *Beyond the Cold War,* "By conditioning military and political élites, on both sides, to act in accord with the first premise of adversary posture—to seek ceaselessly for advantage and to expect annihilating attack upon the first sign of weakness—[strategic doctrine] could tempt one side (if a manifest advantage should arise) to behave as theory prescribes, and to seize the opportunity for a preemptive strike. And what would the war, then, have been *about*? It would have been about fulfilling a theorem in deterrence theory." It's a striking historical fact, and one that should make us reflect, that the severest crisis of the nuclear age, the Cuban missile crisis, was *about* the weapons themselves.

In truth, there is much evidence that contradicts the pessimistic chief assumption of deterrence. Three historical episodes, among many that could be mentioned, can serve as illustration. The first is the behavior of the United States between 1945 and 1949, when it possessed a monopoly of nuclear weapons. The United States not only did not immediately annihilate the Soviet Union but did not even seek any drastic change in Soviet policy—by, for example, using nuclear blackmail to force the Soviet Union out of Eastern Europe. The second episode is the behavior of the Soviet Union between roughly the mid-1950s and the present, during which time it has had complete nuclear superiority over China and has also been in a state of hostility toward China as least as intense as its hostility toward the United States. According to purely theoretical considerations, the Soviet Union has had every reason to launch a preemptive strike against China, for in all likelihood it could destroy China's nuclear forces entirely. Yet it has not launched a preemptive strike. This restraint is all the more telling because it involves a totalitarian country, which is relatively immune to public opinion. The third episode is the behavior of Britain in its recent successful war to regain the Falkland Islands from Argentina. Argentina, which is not a nuclear power (although it is now able to become one), seized territory that was claimed by a nuclear-armed Britain. According to present theory, Britain should at that point have used its absolute nuclear superiority to force Argentine withdrawal. Britain could, for example, have begun with threats; then backed these up by stationing a nuclear-armed submarine within range of Argentina; then set off a demonstration nuclear explosion, perhaps over the sea, or over an unpopulated part of Argentina; then destroyed an Argentine military base with a "small" (Hiroshima-sized) bomb; then destroyed a small city or two; and, finally, blown Argentina off the map (a feat well within the capacity of Britain's nuclear forces, comparatively small though they are). But, as far as I'm aware, the British government did not breathe the merest suggestion that any of these things were remotely possible. What it did do was launch and win a conventional war, at a high cost in lives and in money. It is interesting to speculate on what Britain might have done if it had faced conventional defeat, but the complete lack of any mention of nuclear arms by government spokesmen, during the war or afterward, allows us to suppose that it would have suffered the defeat rather than resort to nuclear weapons. What was equally striking was the failure of outside observers of the war—columnists, diplomats of other countries, and the like—to mention Britain's nuclear arsenal. Somehow, its complete irrelevance to the situation was intuitively assumed by everybody.

These lessons of experience are of great value to the world—especially since they are hopeful. They prove to us, as we try to shape a safer future, that we have more—much, much more—to work with than terror. In our world, there is also courage, trust, prudence, imagination, decency. There is even love. Can it be "realistic" to exclude these proved good qualities of our species from our calculations? To do so would be to libel mankind and cripple our efforts. Indeed, the whole abolition agreement suggested here can be seen as a mere holding operation, giving us time in which these good qualities can be brought to bear on the vast political work that alone can lead to a true and fully satisfactory resolution of the nuclear predicament.

The theorists correctly justify their resort to pure theory on the ground that no experience of a nuclear holocaust is available; but this justification has been stretched too far, for while post-Nagasaki history does not show what starts nuclear hostilities it shows many examples of what does *not* start them. We should become careful students of negative history, inasmuch as the chief aim of our political efforts in the nuclear age must be to see to it that something does *not* happen—

that we do *not* blow ourselves up. High-school students are required to study the "three causes," or the "four causes," of the First World War, or the Second World War, or whatever. We must study the causes of the lack of war—the causes of peace. Leaving the study of "nuclear war" to the theorists, we as historians can study its prevention. One of the first things our study shows us is that, while in theory even slight imbalances in nuclear forces lead to instability and war, in actuality they have not done so. Another thing it shows is that with a war in progress a power possessing a monopoly of nuclear weapons may choose not to use them, or even to remind the world that it possesses them. The statesmen of the nuclear age seem to act with a sobriety not credited to them by our theorists. Some of the assumptions of deterrence theory can never be tested in action (not if we hope to survive), but others can be and have been. Among them is the assumption that nuclear powers will seek out and exploit any nuclear imbalance to obtain political or military advantage. This assumption has now been put to the test of experience many times, and has proved each time to be false. Why did the United States not preemptively attack the Soviet Union in the 1940s? Why has the Soviet Union not preemptively attacked China? Why did Britain choose to expend the lives of its soldiers in the Falkland Islands rather than even rattle its nuclear sword at Argentina? We can only guess at answers. Perhaps in the back of the minds of the leaders of these nations was some notion that what you do to others will one day be done to you. Perhaps they felt that even to threaten a nuclear attack would shame them before the world and history. Perhaps they feared that a nuclear attack of any sort would engulf the world in a chaos in which their own nations would suffer. Or perhaps their consciences stayed their hands.

It would be self-defeating folly to deny the common sense of the central axiom of deterrence—that the fear of nuclear retaliation provides nations with an overwhelming incentive not to launch nuclear attacks—but it would also be folly if, granting that, we concluded that the fear of retaliation was the only sentiment at work in holding the world back from nuclear destruction. So it is not meaningless, after showing that no country could expect to profit by violating an abolition agreement, to point out that even if some statesman mistakenly concluded that his country could profit from aggression he might be restrained for any number of reasons, including the sense of shame and repugnance that almost every human being feels at the thought of murdering millions, and possibly billions, of innocent people in cold blood.

It is in the spirit of seeking to reach a broad judgment, not of trying to produce a whole new crop of scenarios, that I want to address the question of whether or not an abolition agreement would be workable. In the years ahead, a profusion of plans and ideas defining not just steps but whole stairways to nuclear disarmament will, in all likelihood, be put forward as people seek instruments for their newfound will to save the species. At the same time, people will be seeking to understand more profoundly what it means to live in a world in which we have the power to exterminate ourselves. And out of a deepening understanding will come still further thoughts about what we should be doing. For no single plan can guide us. And no single person can possess the wisdom to chart our course. It is in the very nature of things that the effort will be collective. The world is not to be approached, blueprint in hand, as if it were so much raw material waiting to be fashioned to someone's design. *We*—the people of the earth, each of us possessing an independent will—are that material, and it will be only out of the combined resolve of all of us that, probably at unexpected times and in unexpected ways, our will, the will of the world, will make itself known and felt. If the remarks in these pages are not predictions, neither are they would-be blueprints for the future. Rather, they, and the whole proposal for abolition described here, are an attempt to make a contribution to the broader discussion out of which, we must hope, will come the actual steps that lead us away from the abyss.

As the examples of nuclear restraint I have cited demonstrate, there are more motives acting in favor of military restraint in the nuclear age than a simple fear of nuclear retaliation. Strict deterrence theory recognizes only this fear, and disregards all other factors, and it is in that respect like an insurance policy—it deals with the worst case. It offers assurance that even if an aggressor were to disregard all other constraints and try his worst he could not hope for victory. It does not tell us that our adversary *will* try to burn our house down, or even that he necessarily wants to, but only that if this thought ever crosses his mind, and he is rational, he will have cause to dismiss it. Therefore, to whatever extent we fear that the adversary will do his worst, including his nuclear worst, and to whatever extent we are willing in return to do our worst, including our nuclear worst, the assurances offered by credible deterrence are important. To some people, they are all-important. But to someone who, like me, feels that he cannot find a justification for even threatening to use, to say nothing of using, nuclear weapons, in support of either armed or weaponless deterrence, any proposal that relies on a threat to use them, including the proposal for weaponless deterrence, raises an ethical question. I oppose any use of nuclear weapons, whether in a first strike or in a second strike or in any strike at all. But, as I have said, I believe that in dealing with the nuclear predicament we must support interim measures—measures such as the establishment of a Soviet-American control center for the exchange of information in a crisis; SALT or START agreements; a policy of no first use of nuclear weapons; the freeze; reductions in the nuclear arsenals; or the abolition of nuclear arms coupled with weaponless deterrence—that will help steer mankind away from its extinction, even though in the meantime we go on depending on morally obnoxious means. Today, mankind is like a person who lies bleeding to death on the street after an accident. Eventually, this person will require major surgery. But right now he needs to be rushed to the hospital in an ambulance, and given first aid on the way. It is pointless to say at this moment, ''This person doesn't need an ambulance, he needs major surgery.'' The passage from our nuclear-armed world to a nuclear-weaponless world would be that ambulance ride. Once the life of mankind is out of immediate danger, we will have the time—we will have won it for ourselves—to address the radical and sweeping measures of global political renovation which alone can fully deliver us from the evil.

* * *

As we consider whether deterrence could remain in force under an abolition agreement, the work of present-day theorist of deterrence is helpful, because under the agreement the requirements of deterrence would be exactly what they are today. Deterrence would require stability, which would mean that under the system every statesman in his right mind would see that the almost certain result if he launched aggression would be the pointless destruction of all concerned, including, most definitely, his own country; that is, it would require that the hope of military victory vanish from his mind. It would require credibility, which would mean that the ability to visit devastation on an aggressor would have to be secure. It would therefore require a retaliatory nuclear capacity that would survive any first strike the adversary could mount. In connection with these requirements, the most important question to ask about a nuclear-weapon-free world is whether it could be arranged in such a way that no nation, by sudden or surreptitious rearmament, or by military action, could defeat an adversary or blackmail it into submission. (Obviously, the ability to defeat and the ability to blackmail are linked, since no country is going to allow itself to be blackmailed unless the prospect of defeat is virtually certain.) This question is far more complicated than is commonly acknowledged. Usually, it is disposed of in a few sentences that are prefatory to the author's getting down to his real interest, which, typically, is either to discuss the mechanics of armed deterrence or to set forth the provisions for world government. (The near-total lack of interest of each of these schools in the details of the other's thinking is remarkable.)

If the abolition of nuclear weapons were the same as their uninvention, a sudden violation of the agreement (by a nation that had somehow invented them again) would really constitute an insuperable advantage. The violator would then be in the position that the United States was in vis-à-vis Japan in July of 1945. But since abolition is not uninvention, and the intended victim of nuclear blackmail would be able to retaliate in several weeks' time, the imbalance between the violator and his victim would be much less than it at first appears to be. In 1946, as I have mentioned, Brodie pointed out that if the aggressor "must fear retaliation," then "the fact that it destroys its opponent's cities some hours or even days before its own are destroyed may avail it little." A delay of a month or so would make equally little difference. The unimportance of delays is one more of the differences between deterrence and defense. In defense, the shield has to be raised at the moment the sword falls, not a few days later. But the avenging sword of nuclear retaliation is not dulled by a wait. There is, indeed, something awful—something "deterring"—about the prospect of delayed retaliation. It's interesting to ponder whether the United States would have used the atomic bomb against Japan if Japan had been known to be a few weeks away from having one itself (as in fact it was not). Would the United States have been ready to risk New York and Chicago for Hiroshima and Nagasaki? I doubt it. The point in the present context is that the imbalance between a country that has invented the bomb and one that hasn't is categorically greater than the imbalance that exists between two nations that have both developed the bomb but one of which has dismantled its arsenal.

As deterrence theory teaches us, to have a really decisive advantage in a first strike the violator would have to possess forces sufficient to erase the victim's capacity for retaliation. To be really worth anything, therefore, a first strike delivered out of secrecy under an abolition agreement would have to be utterly devastating to the victim's nuclear capacity and be followed up by the immediate and total occupation of the victim's country with conventional forces, in order to prevent its nuclear rearmament. It is perhaps imaginable that if the defenses of the capacity for retaliation were left to chance a determined aggressor could, with the use of concealed arsenals only, so thoroughly devastate and then so swiftly occupy its victim that the victim could not retaliate. However, the defenses of the retaliatory capacity would not be left to chance. Rather, under the abolition agreement not only would the readiness to rebuild nuclear weapons be in place but so would the anti-nuclear defenses and the defensively arrayed conventional forces. The violator's aggression would fail, because the abolition agreement would have been *designed* for it to fail. Under this agreement, whatever is necessary to defeat such aggression would be built in, probably redundantly, for the sake of everyone's peace of mind.

The question of the state of readiness for nuclear rearmament is complex. It would have to meet two basic requirements. First, it would have to permit a lead time long enough to be of real benefit to the world. (Yet any increase would be beneficial. For example, if the nuclear powers today did nothing more than remove the nuclear warheads from their missiles and store them nearby, so that it would take, say, six hours to put them in again, the gain would be great. It would increase the lead time by several thousand per cent.) Second, it would have to provide a smooth and assured path back to nuclear armament, in order to fulfill the need, as it is defined by deterrence theory, for the retaliatory force to be invulnerable. In all likelihood, the best way of providing such a path while at the same time lengthening the lead time would be to establish controls on fissionable materials. A more radical measure would be to ban nuclear reactors in general (probably with certain narrowly defined exceptions), or else to place them—as the Baruch Plan, proposed by the United States to the United Nations in 1946, did—under the control of an international body. Banning reactors would carry a higher economic cost, but it would provide a longer lead time, and it might be more easily verifiable, since nuclear reactors and the industry that builds and maintains them are a great deal more difficult to hide than bombs or delivery vehicles. Another set of provisions could cover delivery vehicles. Since any vehicle, whether it is a missile or the suitcase carried by a pedestrian, can be a delivery vehicle for nuclear weapons, removing delivery vehicles for nuclear weapons from the world forever is impossible, just as removing forever the ability to build the weapons themselves is impossible. The important, attainable goal would be to restrict national capacities for deploying delivery vehicles, much as nuclear-arms-control agreements attempt to do today.

Clearly, the complexity of the nuclear balance at the level of zero weapons would be great—though not, perhaps, as great as the complexity is today, with thousands of weapons and their varied delivery systems in existence. The decisions to be made would have to deal not only with the state of readiness to rearm but also with the extent of the technical means permitted, its deployment, and so on. For example, it would be an advantage to the agreement as a whole if the technical means were decentralized to begin with and, in addition, were further dispersible in the event of the agreement's breakdown. (In the agreement, a nation's right to rearm if an adversary had done so would, of course, be recognized.) Dispersibility, in particular, would be invaluable. It could suffice in itself to defeat nuclear blackmail by a violator of the agreement. Blackmail requires that a threat be openly made and that time be allowed for compliance with its demands. But that time could be used to disperse the technical means from their known and inspected places to secret places. Once dispersal had occurred, it would be impossible for the small, secretly assembled nuclear force of the violator to threaten the retaliatory capacity of the victim. The question of what to do if the abolition agreement should be violated would be analogous to the question today of what to do "if deterrence fails." But whereas today we cannot think of one single thing that it would make sense to do if deterrence fails, there would be many sensible things to do if the abolition agreement broken down, including beginning to rearm. To be sure, if the violations continued to grow, and the world began to return to full armament, the actions in response would start to make less and less sense. Yet, even as they continued, the world would have time—as it would not today "if deterrence fails"—to see where it was heading, to reflect, and to pull back.

The principal mission of the anti-nuclear defensive forces set forth in the agreement would be not to protect their nations—a task that in the long run they could perform no better than they can today—but to protect the retaliatory capacity as it was being mobilized for action. They would thus have the limited role of a hedge against cheating. For the defensive superiority that was arranged for in the abolition agreement would last only as long as that agreement did—or, rather, as long afterward as the defensive retained the upper hand. And this would not be indefinitely. It would be only long enough for the attacked nation to assemble its retaliatory force, at which point the balance of terror as we know it today would be restored. But, of course, just as today we keep our retaliatory force at the ready in the hope that its very existence will prevent the attack that would cause us to use it, so in a world of zero nuclear weapons we would preserve our well-defended readiness to rearm in the hope that it would prevent the rearmament that would lead us to rearm. Thus, although we would be relying provisionally on defense we would still be living in a deterred world. Defense would provide protection while the deterrent forces were assembled, but then deterrence would take over. The underlying facts of life in a nuclear-weapon-free world would be just what they are today—that defense is impossible and deterrence inescapable. And under deterrence, armed or unarmed, our hope is that deterrence itself would gradually become obsolete while the conditions for a real, full peace were being established. Our chief protection, then, which would operate before either defenses or deterrence was called into play, would be whatever political will we had mustered to institute, and then to uphold, the abolition agreement.

None of this is to say that defense of the population should be ruled out. The question of whether or not to deploy civil defense, as a further hedge against cheating, is debatable. It could be argued (as it is today by the advocates of deterrence) that civil defense, if it could be made to work (as it can't today, in the face of our giant nuclear arsenals), would be destabilizing, because it would erode the "effectiveness" of the foe's retaliatory capacity. With an abolition agreement in force, however, the world would not be *counting* on cheating; it would be trying to discourage it, and in that effort protection of the population would be helpful, because it would reduce the effectiveness of blackmail. In general, defensive measures would constitute a sort of obstacle that would-be aggressors would know that they had to overcome before their aggression began to pay off. But since they would also know that before that moment came their intended victims would have armed themselves with nuclear weapons, in preparation for retaliation, the moment would actually never come, and they would abandon their aggressive plans.

A provision for a balance in conventional forces would be essential to the agreement as a whole, because it would prevent the nuclear-arms race from being replaced by a conventional-arms race. "Conventional" arms today are in fact anything but that. Though they are overshadowed by nuclear weapons, they have increased in destructive power to a point at which the doctrine of mutual assured destruction might be maintained by them alone—especially when biological and chemical weapons are taken into account. The principal strategic mission of these limited and balanced conventional forces would be to do their part in deterring a disarming first strike by a violator of the agreement. Since to be successful in preventing nuclear rearmament and retaliation such a strike would require full occupation of the attacked country, the conventional forces would be deployed to prevent invasion. But this would be so in two senses: they would be armed in such a way that they *could* repel an invasion by another country, yet they would be armed in such a way that they *could not* themselves invade another country. These armies would, for example, be loaded down with anti-tank weapons but low on tanks; well equipped with anti-aircraft weapons but ill equipped with aircraft. The present Swiss Army, which bristles with weapons to repel invaders but itself never invades anybody, might serve as a model. Equipping those armies would admittedly be a novel military task but not an impossible one, especially when we remember that all the military planners would be on the same side: the side of defense. Their aim would be to equip every army with steel shields and rubber swords. It is only a little bit facetious to suggest that the two sides might establish a joint "defense department" (properly named, for once), devoted to the development of defensive weaponry. A new "arms race" would begin, between offensive and defensive arms, but, fortunately, all the nations of the world would be working together to support the defense.

The preservation on both sides of an ability to rebuild nuclear weapons, arrangements for inspection on whatever level was necessary to provide a safeguard against cheating, and the presence of limited and balanced conventional forces defensively arrayed would, it seems to me, be more than adequate to provide for the requirements of deterrence in a world without nuclear weapons. Each of these elements would exist in a balance with the others. For example, an estimate would be needed of how much cheating might be possible under a particular level of inspection. When the estimate was given, the deployment of the capacity for rearming would be adjusted to meet, or more than meet, that potential threat. As more inspection was made possible, the less ready the capacity for rearming would have to be, and the less extensive the defense would have to be (although it seems that there would be little to be lost in making defenses redundant). Every advance in inspection, then, would permit a lengthening of the world's nuclear fuse, and an increase in the world's safety. For example—to pick arbitrary figures—if the estimated amount of conceivable cheating associated with a particular level of inspection was a hundred bombs on a hundred commercial airliners, then the level of readiness could be quite low and the needed defenses quite thin. If, however, the estimated amount of conceivable cheating was two hundred bombs on two hundred cruise missiles, then the readiness would have to be higher and the defenses stronger. Conversely, the better the defenses were, the less strict the inspection would have to be. And, of course, the precise technical form of the agreed-upon readiness to rearm would have a bearing on how effective the defense of it could be. The important point in the present context is that the levels of inspection, of readiness, and of defense are interdependent and adjustable, with considerable room for margins of safety to be built in when the abolition agreement is designed.

The difficulties facing a violator of an abolition agreement only multiply when one turns from purely technical considerations to strategic ones. Let us suppose that a violator of the agreement has assembled a clandestine nuclear arsenal. But an arsenal is not in itself a policy. How to gain a military or political advantage from it remains to be figured out. To begin with, the cheater has to take into account the possibility that its intended victim has cheated as well. The possibility of cheating cuts two ways: it permits violation of the agreement, but it also sows suspicion in the mind of the would-be cheater that the other side may have cheated, too. Those who cheat know from their own action that cheating is possible, and are likely to suppose that others have done it also. If that has happened, the cheater, when he pulls back the curtain of secrecy, reveals the hidden arsenal, and starts making demands, will find himself facing an opposing arsenal right away, and the exercise will be fruitless. In short, uncertainty about cheating can have a deterrent as well as a destabilizing effect. (Uncertainty, it seems, is in all circumstances the most steadfast ally of deterrence.)

A cheater might have either of two possible aims: to hedge against suspected cheating on the other side or to engage in aggression. If the aim was to secure a hedge, then the cheating, while dangerous and undesirable, would remain clandestine and without disastrous consequences. (This would be so even if it had occurred on both sides, because then, although nobody would know it, a nuclear balance would have been created, at very low levels of armament.) There is reason to believe, however, that nations would not find it in their interest to cheat even as a hedge. The protective benefit of the hedge would be offset by the extremely serious cost of being in a violation. When one considers that in order to act as a hedge a violation would have to continue indefinitely, and therefore discovery would be likely sooner or later, it is hard to imagine that a nation would find it worthwhile—especially if it knew that in the event of a violation by another nation its legitimate capacity to rearm was secure. If, on the other hand, the aim was aggression, then the violator would face all the defensive and retaliatory penalties that are built into the agreement to deter aggression. And yet, even without considering these, the government leader weighing the costs of cheating would have to reflect that his victim, or one of his victims's allies, might have cheated, and that in that case his plans would be aborted right there. In other words, the violator, after revealing himself to the world as an international outlaw of the most hateful and terrifying kind, might be thwarted immediately, without having a chance even to attempt some mischief in a brief moment of nuclear superiority.

In the event that a government overlooked all these obstacles and decided that it was ready to violate the agreement anyway, it would still need a strategy. It would have to have both an attainable political goal in mind and a plan for reaching it. Neither is easy to conceive of. Just as is true in our present world, the strategy for a first strike, whether only threatened or actually carried out, would have to be, in the jargon terms, either ''counterforce'' or ''countervalue''; that is, the bombs would have to menace or destroy either the foe's military forces, in the hope of achieving a crippling first strike, or the foe's cities and population, in the hope of terrorizing him into submission. A successful counterforce strike would be impossible for all the reasons just mentioned; the entire abolition agreement would have been framed to preclude it. The idea, for example, that the Soviet Union, using a clandestine nuclear force, could destroy the ability of the United States to make nuclear weapons and then, in the space of a few weeks, conquer Europe, cross the Atlantic, and occupy the United States to prevent nuclear rearmament is patent fantasy. And if one adds that the first strike with the clandestine arsenal would be opposed by large-scale defenses, including swift dispersal of the nuclear weapon-making capacity, and that the conventional forces of the Soviet Union had, under the agreement, been reduced from their present size and deprived of many of their offensive arms, then the idea of such an attack positively enters the realm of the surreal. That would leave the possibility of blackmail against cities or actual attacks on them—a possibility that is often pointed to as the decisive advantage of violating an abolition agreement. Such a threat or attack, however, would be even easier than the counterforce one to reply to. In the first place, the elaborate and technically advanced defenses of the victim might be adequate to actually defend in considerable measure against a threat made with the small, probably technically backward offensive forces of the aggressor. But even if the defenses were inadequate the victim's ability to retaliate with nuclear arms in a few weeks' time would erase the aggressor's advantage. The response of the threatened country would be exactly what it is today: it would threaten nuclear attack in return. Deterrence would be fully in force.

It is not, however, until one turns from the methods of a violator to his possible political goals that the ground for believing in the stability of a nuclear-weapon-free world stands fully revealed. The traditional nightmare of global politics is that some single nation or bloc will grow so strong that it will upset the balance of power and then move to dominate all the other nations. The Romans once did it. In more recent times, Napoleon and Hitler came close. This larger possibility, standing in the background of smaller crises, can give even minor aggression, when it is launched by a great power, a momentous importance. It also provides the temptation that lures a statesman with grandiose longings onto the path of conquest. When nations are faced with such aggression, the question that their leaders always have to ask themselves is where it will be stopped if not in the instance at hand. This is the famed "lesson of Munich," learned from the experience of France and England in 1938, when, at a meeting with Hitler in Munich, they agreed, essentially, that, rather than go to war with him, they would let him take over Czechoslovakia—only to find that they had to go to war with him anyway a short while later. It is the lesson, too, that is embodied in the so-called domino theory, of more recent times, which holds that aggression must be prevented at the earliest possible moment or it will run out of control and engulf everything. The wedding of this lesson to the doctrine of deterrence is what has led to the disproportion of means and ends in our current military strategy—forcing us to defend, say, the Persian Gulf by, in effect, risking the end of the world. The reason our statesmen are willing to risk the end of the world to protect the Persian Gulf is not that the Persian Gulf is so important (its oil *is* very important, of course, but not worth the extinction of mankind); it is that they are persuaded that if aggression is permitted there—or almost anywhere—

it cannot be stopped later. The leader we fear—the one we build nuclear arsenals to deter—is not the one who wants to grab a disputed piece of territory from his neighbor but the one whose dreams are filled with triumphal visits to subjugated foreign capitals. (Hitler's early-morning visit to Paris in 1940, captured on film by his propagandists, comes to mind.) Our nation's leaders believe that Soviet leaders are determined to dominate the world and will actually do it if they are not stopped in an early stage. The Soviet leaders have reciprocal fears. It may be that in fact neither nation has these unlimited ambitions, but since each believes that the other has them both base their foreign policies on the conviction.

A precise way of posing the question of the stability of a nuclear-weapon-free world is to ask how such a would-be world conqueror might fare in it. I have argued that even the very first step, in which the aspiring Caesar of our time, having nursed his dream of world conquest behind a veil of feigned peacefulness, whipped back the curtain of secrecy, displayed his arsenal to the world, and demanded some political prize, on pain of nuclear devastation if it was denied, would meet with failure—and not for just one reason but for many, redundant reasons—and that, furthermore, he would know this before he started, and would not start. But what is even surer is that if this first act of aggression somehow occurred and was successful it could have no sequel. For before it had been completed it would have set in motion all over the world the countermeasures that would prevent any repetition: not only the victimized nation but every other nuclear-capable nation in the world could rearm with nuclear weapons to confront the violator. And our budding Caesar would know all this, too: if he couldn't figure it out for himself, people would tell him. To an extent perhaps not yet fully appreciated, the development of nuclear arms has provided a surefire antidote to the world's ancient nightmare of military conquest by a single power. Such grandiose ambitions cannot be realized in our world, nor could they be in the world of an abolition agreement. The reason is not that nations are less ambitious or less ruthless than they were in the past; it is that the world has changed. And in this changed world it is not the physical existence of nuclear arsenals but the knowledge of how to build them that is fundamental.

It could be said that this knowledge, which is destined to spread over the whole globe, is like a quicksand in which the feet of the armies of the great powers are sunk. And the reason is deterrence, in the broadest sense of the word: no one wants to embark on an obviously self-defeating enterprise. In our strategic thinking, we seem to have become mesmerized by numbers, speaking easily of a thousand, ten thousand, fifty thousand nuclear weapons. But in reality just ten of them—which can carry the explosive force of *ten thousand* Hiroshimas—provide a level of destructive power outside all historical experience. What government leader in his right mind, knowing that these weapons are available to his enemies, can dream of the military conquest of the world? At best, the great powers can fight desultory, drawn-out, small wars—often unsuccessful— against non-nuclear-armed local peoples (the North Vietnamese, the Afghans). Never again can they sweep victoriously from nation to nation, as the armies of the great conquerors of the past did. They know what likely fate awaits them if they try: some justly infuriated enemy will let off the E in the m of few kilograms of plutonium, multiplied by c^2, and their armies will go up in a puff of vapor. You can't conquer the world with vapor armies. Regrettably, none of this means that nuclear weapons will not be used; it means only that they are unlikely to be used in the service of premeditated schemes of conquest or aggression. Their use, if it occurs, is likely to come by accident, or in the confusion and misunderstanding of a crisis, in which neither side is ready to back down. In a way, it is the very existence of the arsenals, rather than any intention to use them, that makes their use possible. As long as they exist, they can be used. And the moment we abolished them the chances of their use, although still present, would become comfortingly small.

Paradoxically, the anachronism of campaigns of world conquest in the nuclear age might emerge into view more clearly in a nuclear-weapon-free world than it does in our nuclear-armed world. Precisely because our present arsenals are so immense and no government leader can be assured that if he sets off one nuclear bomb they will not all go off, a shadow of doubt hangs over the threat of their use as a means of preventing aggression, and it seems conceivable (though very far from likely, once we think about it) that some power might get away with a serious act of aggression. In a nuclear-weapon-free world, however, with no preposterously overstocked arsenals ready to go off the moment a single bomb was used, the threatened nuclear retaliation for aggression would be less irrational and more "credible." To put it in terms of present strategy, "flexible response" would come into its own, for the self-paralysis that results from our natural reluctance to "defend" ourselves by taking steps that might start an unstoppable slide to the end of the world would no longer occur. Because in a nuclear-weapon-free world the path of aggression and rearmament would be broken into steps, we could see with greater clarity than we can today that every escalation of aggression—every crossing of a new national border—could be met with fully commensurate retaliation.

A further bar to world conquest deserves mention, though it is not nuclear in origin. Throughout our century, local people, inspired by an aroused national consciousness and by patriotic feeling, have put up increasingly strong, and increasingly successful, resistance to foreign domination. Whatever other political principles people may subscribe to, they appear to be mightily determined to take charge of their countries. In our world, the "dominoes" have taken on a life of their own and are in rebellion against the players. The classical empires of the West have been effectively dissolved by this force, and so has the somewhat later Soviet aim of a Communist world revolution under Soviet leadership—today it is virtually a dead letter. Whatever atrocities people may suffer, it seems, they want to suffer at the hands of their own monsters and madmen. More and more, we live in a world in which local people rule in their own places. The single great exception to this local takeover from great powers is in Eastern Europe, where the continued Soviet domination is ultimately maintained by occupying armies. But even there local resistance—especially in Poland—though it is not yet intense enough to expel the Soviets, makes one wonder how long this anachronistic form of political control can last. Today, even the greatest powers must think many times before embarking on a Vietnam or an Afghanistan. For this reason alone, quite apart from the influence of nuclear weapons, world domination by a single power has now become unthinkable. Thus, the ambitions of the great powers are doubly checked: while their nuclear forces are immobilized in the balance of nuclear terror, their conventional armies sink in the swamps of local resistance.

The abolition agreement might be accompanied by collective-security agreements, designed to make the fate of aggressors still clearer to any statesmen who were having trouble perceiving the realities of the world they lived in. Weaponless deterrence would not require collective-security agreements in order to work, but it would lend itself naturally to them and would be strengthened by them. The abolition of nuclear arms would be a militarily equalizing measure. With a number of the technically competent nations standing at the same starting line (the agreed-upon readiness) in any race to rearm, their power would be more nearly equal— at least, in the short run—than it is today. This relative equality would give added importance to alliances. There would be safety in numbers, for even if the potential violator should think that he could escape retaliation by his immediate victim he would know that he could not escape it from a dozen or so nations to which the victim was allied in a collective-security agreement. In our nuclear-armed world, proliferation—of capacity, not of weapons—could be stabilizing. It would multiply the reasons for holding back from aggression. (It's interesting that at least one nation that is now nuclear-capable—India—has forgone actual construction of a nuclear arsenal. Its leaders may count it sufficient that their adversaries know that they *can* build the weapons if they want to.) Of all the developments occurring today, proliferation of nuclear weapons may well be the most dangerous. It raises the possibility that sooner or later a madman may have everyone's fate in his hands. An abolition agreement would not fully insure against this terrifying prospect, but it would give us incomparably more security against it than we have now.

Everyone agrees that nations want to survive, and we can be sure that, given the opportunity, they will take steps to assure their survival. Today, however, there are few steps that any but the two most powerful nations can take to protect themselves from the worst fate of all—annihilation in a general holocaust. All the others must simply wait and watch as their life or death is decided by a few men in Washington and Moscow. In a nuclear-weapon-free world, a field of action would open to them. In peace-time, they could work diplomatically and politically to strengthen the abolition agreement. A good way to begin would be with collective-security agreements. But even if nuclear aggression or nuclear blackmail should be attemped there would still be time to act. There would be an interval of some weeks between the original act of aggression and any nuclear response, and in that period pressures of all kinds—including the pressure of the threat of nuclear retaliation by any number of nations—could be exerted to resolve the crisis. These courses of action could be spelled out in advance, so that any would-be aggressor would be able to see clearly what was in store for him.

In judging a system of deterrence, one needs to concentrate on the train of thought that one believes would run through the mind of any national leader inclined toward aggression. In a nuclear-weapon-free world of the kind I have described, a would-be world conqueror contemplating the technical, strategic, and political consequences of aggression would see, I suggest, nothing but a vast field of insurmountable obstacles and, at the end of it—or even quite early—the same mutual assured destruction that we see today when we contemplate "nuclear war." The nuclear world is unconquerable. The peoples of the world refuse to be subjugated, and they have the means, including—in a world in which twentieth-century physics is an open book to all comers—the nuclear means, to prevent their subjugation. Where once a smooth plain stretched before the conqueror's eye, a would-be conqueror today looks out over a terrain that, like one of those glaciers high in the mountains which claim the lives of climbers, is crisscrossed with slippery crevasses, any one of which can prove fatal. Every step courts suicide. The tiny split atom yawns to swallow him up. One might just as well try to cross the desert in a sailing ship or cross the ocean in a tank as try to conquer the nuclear world with military force. And the abolition of nuclear arms would not change this outlook in any basic way. In the foreground of the nuclear-weapon-free world would be the victim's capacity for rearming, itself protected by powerful defensive forces. Beyond that, would be the nuclear capacity of the victim's allies, and, beyond that, the nuclear and other retaliatory capacities of the whole world, enraged that it had been pushed back toward its doom by the violator, and possessing both the will and the means to resist further aggression. And, finally, there would be the ferocious local resistance of the people of the earth to subjugation: fifty, a hundred, two hundred Vietnams. The potential violator would see that even his first step was extremely unlikely to succeed, the second step impossible, the third pure fantasy. And, seeing all that, he would not take the first step. He would be deterred.

We fear cheating under an abolition agreement because we fear aggression; we fear aggression primarily because we fear that it will upset the balance of power; and we fear an upset of the balance of power because we fear that some single nation or bloc will gain irresistible military superiority and, with it, domination of the world. But in the nuclear world, whether armed or unarmed, these things cannot happen—not because cheating is impossible but because the entire military and political organization of the world in which cheating might have been the first step toward world domination has passed away. No balance of power—only a balance of terror, which is something different. In a balance of power, each side faces the *power* of the other—power to achieve victory in war, to conquer and occupy other countries or the world—but in the balance of terror all *power* has evaporated, and the two sides are impotent in the face of the same oblivion: not anyone's victory or domination but unlimited and universal defeat; not a foe having its way with the world but the end of the world. All human powers are overmatched by the universal power that was unleashed in the world when the atom was split, and that universal power is what, in the final analysis, checks the would-be world conqueror at every step, including the step in which his maniacal dream might crystallize in his brain. When it turned out that E equals mc^2, his sort was doomed. The dreams of world conquest are dead dreams. They belong to a world that has vanished. Its ways and practices—the marching and retreating armies, the contest for "control of the seas" or "control of the air," the long strings of victories and defeats, spanning the continents, and all the rest of the moves and countermoves, the noise and the fire, of those great global pitched battles by which in the pre-nuclear world the political fortunes of mankind were settled—have, like the lances, armor, and escutcheons of feudalism, sunk under the waves of time forever. We cannot get that world back. Yet its loss can be our gain, for we can profit from it as we turn to face the real peril that has been put before us: the featureless, timeless nothingness of our doom.

In political affairs, it's a great advantage to be able to start with what is in place and improve on it, rather than to have to start over. An agreement freezing the world's boundaries in place and abolishing nuclear arms while keeping deterrence in force by retaining the ability to rebuild them offers this advantage. It would be a logical, evolutionary outgrowth of present-day deterrence. Deterrence is built on the foundation of the world's horror at the idea of either suffering a nuclear holocaust or, for that matter, perpetrating one. The abolition agreement would build a stronger and more effective policy on that same foundation. It would be a more reliable, more rational, and (within regrettably defined limits) more humane way of profiting from our horror. Under it, the rationale that the only sensible role for nuclear weapons is to guarantee that those same weapons are never used would not, it is true, be fully carried through to its logical conclusion, but it would be buttressed and strengthened. The latent agreement among adversaries on which deterrence depends would be made explicit and *acted upon*. Their de facto acceptance of the status quo would be institutionalized. Nations would still, in the last analysis, rely on their own nuclear capacities to preserve their independence. But the grotesque disproportion between the causes and the results of "war"—the threat to end the world so as to prevent every threat to the status quo—would be greatly reduced (although not yet removed).

The precise steps by which abolition might be reached would be the product of negotiations, but the most important stage in the great powers' negotiations would consist of an initial formal affirmation and definition, in technical, military, and political terms, of the goal. Agreement on the goal would have to come first because it is impossible to decide on precise steps until one knows where one is heading. At present, strangely, our procedure is the reverse. We concentrate all our energy on the steps (SALT, START, the freeze, and so on), and simply leave unanswered the question of where all this is going. (At the moment, it seems to be going nowhere.) Is our aim the stability of existing arsenals? Is it President Reagan's defensive world, protected from nuclear attack by weapons in space and elsewhere? Is it "reductions"? "Deep reductions"? If so, how deep? Down to "minimum deterrence"? What then? Or do we—as a number of Presidents, including President Carter and President Reagan, have hinted—seek abolition? If we do, what is the world going to look like then, and what are we going to do if trouble starts? Up to now, these questions have somehow been seen as unfit for government to answer. In this matter—the most important matter of all—government has been content to grope along a path that lacks a clearly defined destination. Even the peace movement has been shy about advocating full nuclear disarmament—showing a reluctance as crippling to its cause as hesitation to advocate the abolition of slavery would have been to that of the anti-slavery movement. The answer one gives to the question of the goal determines the character of the steps one takes. And the lack of an answer—of a destination for arms control—means that the steps falter, grow uncertain, cross back over each other, and finally stop. With no consensus in place on where we are going, policy shifts from Administration to Administration; and even within each Administration there is a lack of clarity about what would be desirable. The general public, for its part, is left in total confusion, unable to bring its will to bear, or even to form its will, on questions of specific policy. One Administration concentrates on delivery systems, another on throw-weight and numbers of warheads. Two Presidents say that they seek abolition, and Harvard and the *New York Times* say that abolition is impossible. One President sees anti-nuclear defenses as injurious to stability, and the next sees them as the key to stability. One school of expert thought says that the stabilization of forces, even at something like present levels, should be the goal of arms control, and another school thinks that reductions should be the goal. The point here is not so much to argue that any of these views is right or wrong per se as to suggest that without agreement on a single, clear goal for arms control we have no standard by which to measure anyone's views.

A clear goal, once adopted, would serve as an organizing principle for both our steps and our ideas. If after study our government adopted abolition as its goal—not as a rhetorical flourish for the peroration of presidential speeches but as a practical, thought-out destination—many points currently under discussion would be clarified. The issue of anti-nuclear defenses is a case in point. As we have seen, such defenses are destabilizing *before* an abolition agreement (because they only spur increased offensive measures on the other side) but become stabilizing *after* an abolition agreement (as a hedge against cheating). Thus, until the great powers were well on their way to abolition we would rein in defenses, but once they were on their way we would encourage defenses. The issue of reductions would also be clarified. Reductions become unambiguously necessary. Because they would be the path leading to zero, they would lose the air of pointlessness that they necessarily have as long as it is believed that mutual assured destruction must be preserved, if only "minimally." (Reductions short of abolition, it should be said, might serve one invaluable purpose: they might—though when we consider the nuclear winter we can't be sure—bring the arsenals down to a level still adequate for mutual assured destruction but not sufficient to cause extinction.) The goal of stability, too, would gain a new context.

Once the goal had been studied, defined, and accepted, the steps, it seems to me, would not be hard to find. Without trying to go into detail, I shall mention a few principles by which they might be established. A basic principle governing the whole process would be that deterrence would remain in effect at every stage, including, of course, the final one—abolition itself. Most important, at every step, all the way down to zero, each side would retain a secure retaliatory capacity. The deterrence theory in use, however, would be "existential deterrence," rather than any of the more theoretically elaborate kinds. Instead of being guided by detailed scenarios of possible nuclear wars, we would rely on common sense and the lessons of history, which show that nations are even more reluctant to use nuclear weapons than deterrence theory suggests. Guided by this rough-and-ready version of deterrence, which, though it is less intellectually dazzling than some of the others, corresponds better to our actual, fallible human predictive powers, the negotiating partners would seek a balance at all stages of the reductions but would not get unduly alarmed if imbalances appeared in one area or another now and then.

As reductions continued, the capacity for retaliation would consist less and less of the possession of weapons and more and more of the capacity for rebuilding them, until, at the level of zero, that capacity would be all. Indeed, the more closely we look at the zero point the less of a watershed it seems to be. Examined in detail, it reveals a wide range of alternatives, in which the key issue is no longer the number of weapons in existence but the extent of the capacity and the level of readiness for building more. (At even quite high levels of warheads—say, the hundreds—the importance of capacity might eclipse the importance of stockpiles). But there would also be the issue of control of delivery vehicles—an issue that at the zero level might well be even more important than the abolition of warheads. Since the man with a suitcase is a delivery vehicle, attaining "zero delivery systems" is in principle impossible. Instead, the task would be to set specifications for those which were allowed and those which were not. Defining the permissible states of readiness for building the bombs and for building delivery vehicles of various sorts would be the first task of negotiations.

One further strategic notion that would gain depth and meaning in the context of negotiations to establish weaponless deterrence would be the principle of no first use. The value of this concept lies not only in the contribution it makes toward present stability but in its establishment of an almost purely deterrent role for nuclear weapons. (I say "almost" because of the unspoken reservation attached to no first use which specifies that it ceases to apply as soon as one side faces conventional defeat.) If two sides have declared a policy of no first use, then each side possesses its nuclear arsenals only to retaliate in the event that the other side uses them, and since neither side intends ever to strike first neither has any reason to keep its arsenals, and they can be abolished. All that remains is for each side to convince the other that it really *is* abolishing the weapons. When people are persuaded—as so many analysts have been since 1945—that a nuclear-weapon-free world is, in the absence of world government, inherently the least stable of worlds, the opportunity opened up by the two sides' willingness to forswear aggression is lost. But if, as I have argued here, a nuclear-weapon-free world can be stable, with deterrence remaining in effect, then the opportunity can be seized. The no-first-use principle coupled with the principle of achieving weaponless deterrence could provide the foundation for complete nuclear disarmament.

When a person or a society or, as in this case, a whole planet is embarked on a self-destructive and ultimately suicidal course, the first order of business is a decision to *reverse course*. To reverse course is not in itself to arrive at the safe shore, which may still be far in the distance, but it is at least to glimpse that shore and to turn one's craft in its direction. A discussion of what the ultimate aims of the United States' disarmament policy should be, culminating in the actual adoption of a goal, could be the means by which the needed course reversal would take place. The arena in which the debate over the ultimate goals of disarmament takes place should be government, but not government alone. Ideally, it should encompass all of society, but since it is in fact only in the West that free discussion can occur, the debate should begin here. One step in the direction of such a deliberation might be, for example, the appointment of a presidential commission to restudy the whole issue, from the ground up. Another might be for Congress to hold joint hearings on the question—hearings that would be televised in full before the nation. The press, the universities, and the other independent voices in the society could join in. But it may not be necessary for anyone to take any self-conscious steps to start this discussion. When the time is right, it will be unstoppable. Indeed, it may have already begun.

Just as the steps in arms control need to be placed in the context of the abolition of nuclear arms, so abolition needs to be placed in the context of a full resolution of the nuclear predicament. Abolition would not give us a world from which nuclear weapons had been eradicated forever, which is to say that it would not return us to the pre-nuclear world. Nothing can do that. Even in the realm of the possible, however, abolition would be only a halfway house—an interim solution. We sometimes say that we live on the brink of nuclear destruction. But, with no more than a mechanical or human mistake or two between us and the end of the world, it would be more accurate to say that we are hanging by one arm from a branch that sticks out over the brink. Abolition would get us up onto the brink. It would get us onto solid ground, where we would have the time and the peace of mind to look at the lay of the land and plan our next steps. Or, to change the metaphor, it would be like reaching a base camp, from which we could reconnoitre to plan the ascent of the mountain itself. To us now, who are unable to restrain ourselves from heaping up more and more nuclear weapons until we hardly know where to deploy them, abolition looks like the peak of Mount Everest. But when we got there we would find that we had climbed only a foothill, and that the real Everest—the political challenge of finding peaceful means for handling all disputes in the international sphere—still rose up before us.

It is tempting to suppose that a nuclear-weapon-free world of stalemated sovereign states could be long-lasting, or even permanent. To resort to one more metaphor, nations in the state of deterrence are like trains on the tracks of a roundhouse, all of which converge upon a central point, like the spokes of a wheel. Let us imagine that reaching the central point would give the engineer of any one train, if he rushed forward with his train and seized it, the means to control all the other trains ("world domination"). To prevent this the engineers resolve that if they see any engineer rushing his train toward the center they will all do the same, destroying the first train and themselves in a single huge collision. But now let us suppose that these tracks extend outward indefinitely, that the trains have all retreated miles into the countryside, and that, furthermore, the engineers have voluntarily entered into a solemn agreement not to come within a defined distance of the center. This, it seems to me, is a fair representation of weaponless deterrence. In recognition of the futility of the resort to force in the nuclear age, nations would have pulled far back from the abyss. The agreement would be their first line of defense against threats both to their national sovereignty and to human survival. They would bend their efforts to preserve it. Yet ultimately they would still rely on the nuclear threat. The engineers are deep in the quiet of the countryside, but if, against all expectation and all reason, one of their number starts rushing toward the central point they are able and ready to do likewise. If we suppose, however, that they manage to stay in their pulled back state long enough—say, centuries—then we can entertain the hope that something like permanence has been achieved. Theoretically, the trains are ready to rush suicidally to the central point, but actually they have, more and more, been conducting relations along branch lines that they have been building up. The whole business of crashing into each other at the central point has gradually become fantastic and unreal—a nightmare from a barbaric and insane past. The converging tracks fall into disuse and become overgrown. Then one day, perhaps, this paraphernalia of mass destruction can be carted off to village greens, to take its place alongside the naval cannons of the past, and to be played on by small children.

But life is movement and change. No stalemate can be eternal. Differences must arise. They will have to be resolved, and a means of resolving them will have to be found—a means other than violence. And then we are faced again with the revolution in our political affairs which some called for in the mid-1940s but which never happened. At issue in this revolution would be not just the outcome of one dispute or another—not even the outcome of the East-West struggle in its entirety—but how all nations were to conduct their political relations with one another from then on. Some observers have suggested that, given the limits of what we can hope to accomplish in the near future, it is meaningless to define the predicament in such broad terms. But it seems to me that even while we recognize these limits it is an essential element of honesty for us to measure our accomplishments not against what we have decided it is possible for us to do at a particular moment but against the objective magnitude of the task that, without our willing it or wanting it, has actually been imposed on us by nuclear weapons. This is the first requirement of realism in the nuclear age, and, I believe, it is in a spirit of realism that we should acknowledge that the abolition of nuclear weapons would be only a preliminary to getting down to the more substantial political work that lies ahead. The size of the predicament is not ours to choose; only the resolution is.

The resolution of the nuclear predicament as a whole, then, would fall into two broad stages. In the first (discussed here), the world would, by agreement, institutionalize the broad global stalemate that we are already in, and abolish nuclear weapons. Political changes would still occur, but no longer by military means. In this stage, the differences between nations would not be taken up and resolved but suppressed and postponed. The nuclear peril would still exist in our affairs, but passively. Nuclear weapons would not, by virtue of this arrangement, have become anachronistic, but to whatever extent we took advantage of the respite by finding diplomatic and political means for conducting the world's business peacefully we would *make* them anachronistic. And that process of invention and construction would constitute the second stage (not discussed here) of the resolution of the nuclear predicament. In it, the frozen world of deterrence would begin to melt and move—peacefully—as new, nonviolent means for decision-making were discovered and instituted. With the critical issue of national security provisionally taken care of, it would no longer be necessary for this political work to take the form of a desperate and unwanted plunge into world government. Instead, the world could deal with its international business step by step—not out of panic that the world was about to end but out of a specific and positive desire to take care of the business at hand. Already the agenda of business calling for such attention is long. It comprises all those matters which come under the heading of "interdependence," including global ecological issues and global economic issues. In these and other areas of international life, "sovereignty" has already dissolved. There is no sovereign power over migratory birds or over migratory capital, either. The current global debt crisis is a case in point. The world needs to institute a peaceful, orderly means of resolving it and other economic crises of its kind, in which the individual interests of nations can be served only to the extent that the common interest of all is attended to first. The resolution of the current debt crisis will not save the world from nuclear weapons. But if those weapons had been abolished, then the resolution of that crisis would be one of the limited steps along the path of global political changes ultimately necessary if we are to put nuclear weapons behind us once and for all.

Abolition backed up by weaponless deterrence would thus crack the link between nuclear disarmament and world government in not just one way but two: first, it would enable abolition to occur without our having to solve the underlying political problems; and, second, it would provide a foundation on which those political problems could be addressed piecemeal and gradually rather than all at once. In a word, it would resolve not the nuclear predicament—something that does require that we pursue the solution of the political question all the way to its revolutionary conclusion—but the problem of timing that was presented when, one July morning in 1945, our quick-thinking scientists handed our slow-moving politicians a device that simultaneously put our species in peril of self-extermination and made nonsense of the system of international relations with which, for better or worse, we had lived since the beginning of history. Abolition in this form would enable us to move swiftly to rescue our species from its desperate, moment-to-moment peril of self-destruction while allowing the political solution to proceed at the much slower pace that such vast work seems almost in the nature of things to require. When we first snap awake to the nearly unbelievable fact that our species is teetering on the edge of its doom, we are moved, like someone who sees a child wandering near the edge of a cliff, to spring forward immediately and save it. Yet as long as everyone—radicals and moderates alike—believed that we could not do this without first establishing world government our impulse was checked. If that requirement is waived, however, then, although the path ahead of us may still be difficult, we are free to obey our impulse and spring forward. In clearing away this obstacle, we would, for the first time since nuclear weapons were developed, stretch a frail bridge across the gap that opened at the onset of the nuclear age between the demands of the present global political system and the demands of survival. This would be the first major step toward bringing our policies back into some semblance of alignment with our scruples, and making our mortally imperilled, broken life well and safe and whole.

It might be objected that arranging to keep the world immobilized in national units unchallengeable from without would be a step away from, not toward, a world community—a step backward, in which such units, instead of passing from the world scene, would become more firmly entrenched than ever. And it is certainly true that this world of weaponless deterrence is the direct opposite of the "world without boundaries" of which so many have dreamed. In fact, in a world of weaponless deterrence boundaries, far from disappearing, would become virtually sacrosanct. The world would, in effect, be crystallized into units unchangeable from without—units in which peoples were sequestered, unable to conquer others but also safe from conquest by others. Yet, seen in another light, this organization of our global affairs, instead of impeding the eventual peaceful arbitration of international disputes, could set the stage for it nicely. If international institutions are ever to acquire real power—power to solve a world debt crisis, power to legislate a law of the sea, power to decide whom the Falkland Islands should belong to—then we want that power to be balanced and checked by local power. The great and growing patriotic feeling in the world today could be the source of that power. A world of intense patriotism would be the hardest sort of world in which to carry out either aggression or repression. It is sometimes said that patriotism is an obstacle to peace, and insofar as it has been used to feed and justify hatred of other peoples it has certainly been that. Yet patriotism, before it curdles into hatred, can be a generous, large-spirited sentiment, which lifts one out of one's private concerns and reinforces one's attachment and devotion to the community in which one lives. It might serve well as a staging ground for building the broader loyalties that we must develop if we are to survive.

A nuclear-weapon-free but conventionally armed and nuclear capable world of sovereign and independent states linked together under an abolition agreement would remain an uneasy, dangerous world. Events in it could veer off in unexpected and unwanted directions. It would be subject to breakdowns of many kinds. One has many questions and doubts. Would some local crisis (and we can be sure there will continue to be many crises) draw the great powers into its vortex, and tempt one or more of them back down the path of rearmament, plunging the world into a mad scramble to get back to mutual assured destruction, or something worse? Would it all unravel—precipitately and catastrophically? Would some stern and resolute power, harboring an aggressive will behind smiles of friendship, suddenly burst forth and attack a peaceful and unsuspecting world? Would the West, breathing a vast sigh of relief at having abolished nuclear weapons, also push them out of mind, and grow complacent and soft, while the Soviet Union, still kept under a harsh discipline by totalitarian rule, remained militant and tough? Would the deterrent effect of mere preparations for nuclear armament be impressive enough to influence the actions of governments—to deter them? Would some power see nuclear disarmament as its opportunity to grab some advantage by launching conventional war? No one can say that these or any number of other disasters are impossible. And even if the system worked exactly as we wanted it to it would remain inherently flawed, because we would still be relying on nuclear weapons for our national defense. We would still be implicated in the intention—somewhere, someday, perhaps—of slaughtering millions of people. Instead of rejecting nuclear destruction categorically, we would still be relying on it. Our "no" to nuclear weapons would still be qualified. That this would be so is one more measure of how small a part of the distance to a full resolution of the nuclear predicament we would have travelled.

Our point of comparison, however, is not a world in which the disputes among nations have melted away or are being settled peacefully. It is today's world, in which in order to preserve a precarious "safety" we think we are obliged to threaten ourselves with doom.

If we were to compare the world of an abolition agreement with the Garden of Eden, we would find it very unsatisfactory—very unstable. (But then the Garden of Eden turned out to be rather "unstable" itself.) But if we compare the world of weaponless deterrence with our present world, we find it to be immeasurably better: the impasse would be broken, and our long and difficult journey to a full resolution could begin. Nuclear weapons *would* be abolished. At first glance, a mere increase in the lead time to nuclear hostilities may seem a disappointingly modest gain to be won from the abolition of nuclear weapons. (It seems more impressive when one remembers that, given the everlastingness of the knowledge of how to build the weapons, an increase in the lead time of one length or another is technically the best we can do.) But in fact the modest increase in lead time—from about seven minutes to a month or six weeks—would mark a revolution in stability. The two most shocking features of our present system for organizing the world are the extreme precariousness of our balance on the nuclear tightrope—a precariousness defined by the short lead time—and the extreme price to be paid "if deterrence fails." In a world of weaponless deterrence, both these features would be removed. Strategic analysts largely agree that the two likeliest causes of a nuclear holocaust are, first, a preemptive strike launched out of fear that the other side would launch one and, second, miscalculation, confusion, panic, or accident (human or technological) in the midst of a crisis. Both perils arise from the presence of the arsenals themselves, and both would vanish with the abolition of the arsenals. Nuclear hostilities could begin only as the result of long premeditation and long preparation leading to cold-blooded aggression out of the blue—a course of action that present analysts regard as the unlikeliest of all causes of nuclear hostilities.

We are concerned with the stability of the nuclear world. The absence of the peril of a preemptive strike and the peril of the accidental or semi-accidental strike in a crisis would lend to a nuclear-weapon-free world a stability that we cannot even dream of in our present world of huge nuclear arsenals. For the same reason, the extremity of the penalty would have been reduced, too. Since there would be no huge arsenals, there would, of course, be no peril that the world would be blown up in an instant. Instead, in the event of a breakdown the number of nuclear weapons used—if any— would be small at first. In our present, abundantly armed world, the gruesome lessons of nuclear experience—of nuclear bombs killing people—could not be brought to bear to save us from the final abyss; once we went over the brink, there would be no hope that, horrified by what we had wrought, we would be able to turn back. But in a nuclear-weapon-free world, the lessons of experience would reinforce deterrence. It would be not only foreknowledge of the horror of nuclear destruction that would stop us from exterminating ourselves but, in the event of a breakdown, the actual spectacle of it. In short, diplomatic and political processes would not be suspended at the brink of nuclear hostilities, as they are likely to be today, but could be continued even after nuclear hostilities had begun. And while there is little hope that these processes could halt a holocaust involving tens of thousands of weapons and lasting a few hours, there is great hope that they could halt one involving hundreds of weapons and lasting weeks or months.

In a recent speech, George Kennan asked, "Can we not at long last cast off our preoccupation with sheer destruction, a preoccupation that is costing us our prosperity and preempting the resources that should go to the solving of our great social problems?" He continued, "For this entire preoccupation with nuclear war is a form of illness. It is morbid in the extreme. There is no hope in it—only horror." Nuclear weapons are truly an evil obsession: they can somehow drag us down even as we try to fight them. They degrade us. They soil us. It is unfortunately true that in a world of unarmed deterrence we would still be relying for our defense on terror—relying for our safety on the threat of terrible crimes. Yet we would have succeeded in pushing the terror and the crimes into the background of our affairs. We would have withdrawn them from the center of the stage, thereby clearing a space into which the peaceful, constructive energies of humanity could flood. But even this retirement of the weapons would not be the most important thing that we had accomplished. It would be that we had made a decision as a species in favor of our survival and then had acted on it. We would have adopted a "deliberate policy"—an unfinished and imperfect one, but a deliberate policy nevertheless. It would not resolve the nuclear predicament, yet the day that the last nuclear weapon on earth was destroyed would be a great day. It would be a day for celebrations. We would have given substance to our choice to create the human future. We would have dispelled once and for all the fatalism and lack of faith in man which, like some dark shadow of extinction itself, have crept over us. And when the celebrations ended, we could turn with new hope and new strength to the unfinished business that lay before us.

INDEX